Slow Down
...and get More
Down
Done

MARSHALL J. COOK

BETTER
WAY
BOOKS

CINCINNATI, OHIO

To Ellen
who taught me to slow down to pet a cat.
She has graced my life with her dreams.

Other fine Betterway Books are available from your local bookstore or direct
from the publisher.

00   99   98   97   96   6   5   4   3   2

Library of Congress Cataloging-in-Publication Data

Cook, Marshall
    Slow down—and get more done / Marshall J. Cook.
        p.   cm.
    Includes bibliographical references and index.
    ISBN 1-55870-270-9
    1. Stress (Psychology) 2. Stress management. 3. Control (Psychology)
        I. Title.
BF575.S75C645   1993
158'.1—dc20   92-39364
                                                                  CIP

Edited by Catherine M. Brohaugh
Desgined by Paul Neff
Cover illustration David Terrill

Betterway Books are available for sales promotions, premiums and fund-raising
use. Special editions or book excerpts can also be created to specification. For
details contact: Special Sales Manager, F&W Publications, 1507 Dana Avenue,
Cincinnati, Ohio 45207.

ACKNOWLEDGMENTS

"Slow down," my father used to tell me. "You'll last longer."

It has taken me a long time to grow into this and the other wisdom my parents have given me. I thank them, my first and best teachers.

I needed a lot of help with this book. Fortunately, I got it.

Thanks to Bill Brohaugh, head honcho at Writer's Digest Books, for believing that we just might have a book here.

Thanks to Dave Fox and Betsy Anderson for helping me work through the concept.

Thanks to Blake Kellogg, who discusses life with me over coffee most every working morning and who gave me particular help with the chapter on creativity, leading me to discover a more appropriate metaphor.

Thanks to Jeremiah Cook, who explores thoughts with me and who helped me focus and temper the chapter on stress.

Thanks to Mary Edwards, who served as a primary source for the material on sleep and dreams and then responded to the chapter as it emerged.

Thanks to Lynn Entine, who led me to a kinder, gentler chapter on exercise and diet.

Thanks to Peter Gilmour for his wise counsel on the discussion of reading.

Thanks to Ellen Cook for guidance throughout and for particular help on the chapter on work.

I've borrowed life stories and insights from lots of good people. I do so with affection and gratitude. Thanks to Dave Ramey, Vern Arendt, Herbert Kubly, John Thiede, Matt Joseph, Clarke Stallworth, Kent Douglass, Shirley Bender, Jill Mork, Jean and George Cook, Dale Cook, Ellen and Jeremiah Cook, Butch Miller, Norbert Blei, Joe Lloyd McAdams, Boomer Clark, Bobbo DaPrato, the good folks of Vega, Texas, Harv Thompson, Barry Levenson, Lindy Bruce and all the others who didn't know they were becoming a part of my book.

About midway through the revision, I realized how much my editor, Catherine Brohaugh, had helped me with this book — and how much her help means to me. She did an amazing job of pulling my material together and helping me make a book of it.

And finally, thanks to Sandy Grieshop, the production editor, whose efforts and insights substantially improved this book.

TABLE OF CONTENTS

Part III: Going slow in a hurry-up world

Part IV: Enjoying the slow-down life

16. Running naked in the streets

How to slow down and become constantly creative.
The secret of creative thinking revealed: Put a lot of bees in
your mental meadow.
How to break down the mental barriers.
Owning it: Making time for fusions.

17. Stress, time and the meaning of life

Finding the courage to overcome speed sickness.
How to unmask your fears and reclaim your right to decide.
Living a values-centered life.
Owning it: Developing your organizing principle.

Bibliography

Books that fed this book.

Index

ABOUT THE AUTHOR

Marshall J. Cook

is a professor at the University of Wisconsin-Madison Outreach, where he teaches workshops on creativity, writing and publishing.

He edits *Creativity Connection*, a quarterly newsletter for writers.

He wrote and self-published *Writing for the Joy of It* (Will Beymer Press, 1990). He has authored *Freeing Your Creativity: A Writer's Guide* and *How to Write With the Skill of a Master and the Genius of a Child* (both for Writer's Digest Books). He has published a couple of hundred magazine articles and short stories in publications ranging from *Law and Order* to *Working Mother*.

Marshall likes to read, talk back to the television, jog and lift weights—not all at the same time—and has written several novels. He's working on another, *The Year of the Buffalo*.

He is married to the former Ellen Malloy, and they have one son, Jeremiah; Rosie, the rogue miniature Schnauzer; and two nearly nose-less Persian cats, Ralph and Norton.

My personal tussle
with time

"Only one person can teach you—yourself."
FREDERICK FRANCK, *THE ZEN OF SEEING*

I'll be preaching to you with all the zeal of the recent convert. Consider this book the observations of a foot-jiggling, horn-honking, caffeine-swilling victim of speed sickness who is slowly getting well.

In twenty years as a professional writer and teacher, I've never missed a deadline. I don't think I've been late for a class or a workshop more than twice—"late" for me meaning "not early"—and I couldn't tell you when those two times might have been. I'm proud of that record. I regard punctuality and reliability as marks of a professional and as a sign of the respect I feel for my editors, my readers and my students. But my punctuality also reflected a near-obsession with time and with filling every waking moment of that time "productively."

I wrote two books on creativity and writing for Writer's Digest Books right before I wrote this one. In both earlier books, I dealt with issues of time and creativity. I discovered that we can't always schedule breakthroughs, that creativity can't be bullied or coerced, that our best ideas often grow out of playing and goofing, that the Big Mind needs time to simmer before yielding its insights. I realized that fatigue and preoccupation, two symptoms of speed sickness, kill inspiration and enthusiasm, and without these great gifts, the struggle is often too hard, the reward too meager.

While spending a couple of hours a day writing my way into discoveries about creativity, I was also trying to be present to my family, meet the demands of my job as an outreach professor for the University of Wisconsin-Madison, keep to a daily exercise schedule, and tend to a freelance magazine writing career. I've always lived at a flat-out sprint, but this frantic schedule made me begin to question the wisdom of life on perpetual fast-forward.

I was driving myself hard, treating myself nowhere near as well as I treat my dog. I went on a diet to lose ten pounds and lost twenty-five instead. A concerned secretary asked if I was okay. I think she was afraid I was dying.

I began to reflect on my approach to time. I read what others have written about it. I talked to successful people who manage to accomplish a great deal without killing themselves in the process. My observations began to grow into this book. They also began to change the way I work and live. I wrote my way into a personal revelation, a new way of dealing with time.

I'm healing. I find myself pulling off the interstate and taking the blue highway, figuratively and literally. I read books about *baseball*, the equivalent, I guess, of riding a snail through a patch of molasses, and a pleasure I once denied myself because I thought such activity was unproductive and self-indulgent (which it most assuredly is, wonderfully so). I'm beginning to treat myself with gentleness and love, and I see this kindness spreading into the way I treat others. I'm learning. It's the work of a lifetime.

I've written this book for myself, then, and also for anyone who, like me, grapples with these sorts of issues:

- how to deal with ever-greater expectations—your own and others'—of how much work and how much play you should accomplish and how much satisfaction and fun you should have
- how to get all those "to do" items checked off the list, or how to feel okay if you don't, or how to make a more reasonable list, or how to throw away the list and still do what really needs doing
- how to cleanse your life of the obligations, shoulds, have-tos, and supposed-to-want-tos that have no meaning or value to you or to the people you really care about
- how to sleep comfortably and wake refreshed
- how to take care of body, mind and spirit
- how to receive satisfaction from work
- how to live a balanced life of work, play and rest
- how to meet life's challenges with energy and enthusiasm
- how to live each moment of your evenings, weekends and vacations

A few observations about you

I don't know anything about you, other than the fact that something moved you to pick up this book and read it this far, but I'll risk an observation based on that fact. Your problem isn't motivation. You're not lazy. I'll bet you're motivated, organized and scheduled, maybe within an inch of insanity. You may feel yourself being squeezed in the time vise, and you're beginning to lose your zest for living. In short, you've got speed sickness.

I'll risk a second observation about you: Whatever you're doing, you're probably doing too much.

As you read and interact with the chapters that follow, learning to slow down and breathe deeply, you'll find yourself becoming more, not less, productive. Somewhere between insanity and inertia, you'll find your healthy pace. And you'll wind up accomplishing more of what really matters to you and enjoying your work and your life more in the process.

If there is any wisdom in this book, this is it:

You can slow down, reclaim your life, and still get everything done that needs doing.

You can probably even get more done, and be happier and healthier.

Big promises. I feel confident in making them, though, because I know the wisdom and the motivation won't come from me. They'll come from you.

You won't have to quit your job, sell your possessions and move into a little cabin in the woods to accomplish these miracles. Ellen and I still live in the city. I still work full time as well as write, and Ellen has dropped out of the world of corporate training just long enough to earn a doctorate, which is not exactly a barefoot stroll through the park. We both work long and hard.

But I have made lots of changes in the way I live that busy life. I've found ways to simplify and quiet my life, to strip it of the nonessentials. I found these ways simply because I started looking for them. I've created opportunities to breathe deeply, to appreciate my life, to revel in the animal joy of being alive, not just on vacations or weekends but several times a day. I've developed a whole new attitude toward waiting at red lights and in long lines at the supermarket.

I'm getting over my speed sickness. You can, too.

Owning it

Deciding what all this means for you

The answers you find in this book will be your answers, not mine. Each chapter will include at least one opportunity for you to reflect on what you've just read and apply it to your life. I can't tell you if or how you should change your life. But you can, and these reflections might help.

If you've read books on time management, please don't worry that I'm about to suggest that you keep detailed time logs, listing every activity in five-minute increments; or time grids; or priority "to-do" lists, rating each activity as "A," "B" or "C." None of the happily productive people I know do these things.

Instead, I suggest that you set aside a notebook for capturing all the observations that bubble up as you read this book. I'll ask a few questions to prompt you, but feel free to ignore mine and answer your own. You'll know which questions to ask, and if you let yourself—yes, if you take the time—you'll find the answers within you. Here are a few questions to get you started.

> Would you like to change anything about the way you handle time?
> What do you do now that you really don't want to do?
> What would happen if you stopped doing it?
> What would you rather be doing?
> Can you start doing at least one of those things now?
> Are you waiting for something to happen before you start doing what you want to do?
> Do you really have to wait?
> What's stopping you from living the way you want to live right now?

Take a few moments now to think about these questions and to write an initial response in your notebook. Carry the notebook with you and jot down other thoughts as they occur to you. Once you start noting these thoughts, you may find that you've loosed a torrent of them, a surging flood that might seem to erode the ground under your feet and threaten to carry you away. Let the thoughts come, and don't worry too much yet about where they might take you. Simply let this writing be your first step in an exploration into the time of your life.

CHAPTER ONE

Jumping off the carousel

"Simplify. Simplify."
HENRY DAVID THOREAU

"Simplify . . . so that your mind will have time to hear its own joy."
HUGH PRATHER

How to recover from speed sickness

As I was walking back from a class this morning, on a beautiful, break-your-heart fall day in Madison, Wisconsin, I almost got run over by a rollerblader. The fellow must have been going forty miles an hour and was dressed like a cross between Zorro and The Flash.

I suppose I should have seen him coming, but I wasn't paying attention. I was, in fact, thinking. There's no law against thinking — yet — but it can get you killed in a country where most folks seem to suffer from a severe case of speed sickness.

We were supposed to be entering the Age of Leisure. Instead we live in the Age of Impatience.

We keep inventing ways to travel faster, but the new ways are never fast enough. Walking was too slow, so we jumped on a horse and dug our heels into the poor, startled creature's sides. The horse soon seemed too pokey, so we developed the horseless carriage and proceeded to build our entire society around it. Never mind that cars kill more of us than any war, and that they poison our air. Those babies can move! In the 1930s, futurists predicted that we'd soon be able to drive across the country in a day. (Of course, they also predicted that we'd be able to control the weather and extract fertilizer from the air.)

We kept developing better roads and raising the speed limits, bypassing main street and then bypassing the bypass. But our roads keep filling up, and we still wind up stuck in traffic, participating in what some sadist dubbed "rush hour."

We bob and weave and honk our horns and generally work ourselves into a fuming fit. We shout at the nincompoop in front of us, while the nincompoop behind us shouts at us. In Seattle recently, a motorist blocked by traffic could stand it no more. She drove her car onto the sidewalk and ran over a pedestrian — three times.

We worship speed and express scorn for "mañana" cultures. We disdain anyone other than the very young or the very old who takes a nap. We like to save time, buy time and gain time. We hate wasting time, killing time and serving time.

We've developed labor-saving devices to give us more time:

- tubes to blend our food before we eat it and to dispose of it if we decide we don't want to eat it
- machines to wash and dry our clothes and dishes
- electric shavers to cut the hairs we don't want and electric combs to tame the ones we do
- power mowers to mow and mulch our lawns and power spreaders to make more lawn grow

The list ends only at the farthest reaches of our ability to invent, build and sell more stuff. But instead of liberating us to do other, presumably more important or more satisfying activities than wash dishes and mow lawns, our possessions have come to possess us. We spend our time buying, maintaining, worrying about and repairing our gadgets; we devote countless hours to making enough money to afford more gadgets. Meantime, time for play and reflection vanishes. And we lose the quiet satisfaction of taking care of ourselves and doing the small, routine jobs that once gave life its texture. (Several friends have told me they occasionally wash dishes the old-fashioned way, with lots of suds and hot water, as a form of therapy when they're upset.)

How time-savers devour time

Most of us seem to feel that we have less and less time to call our own, and that perception has made us increasingly frantic about how we spend that time. So we're easy prey for anyone who promises to save us time. The promise usually involves buying some sort of device that plugs into the wall or runs on batteries.

But it takes time to shop for all those "time-saving" gadgets that are supposed to free us from the drudgery of physical labor. And we're being presented with increasing — and increasingly complex — choices.

Take the telephone—please. You used to buy your phone from The Phone Company and choose between white or black. You were called on to decide nothing more complex than whether to order an extension cord. But now there are several phone companies to choose from, and phones come in a bewildering array of colors, sizes and shapes—from a sneaker to a wine decanter—with your choice allegedly making your "personal statement."

And that's before you begin to consider the optional extras. Should you get an answering machine? Do you need call-waiting? Would a second line somehow enhance your life? How about a phone for the car? And a portable phone so you can talk while mowing the lawn or taking a bath (doing two things at once being the very essence of saving time)?

You know you should read *Consumer Reports* and engage in critical evaluation before you buy (just as you should listen to the candidates debate and read the position papers before you vote). But all that takes time, and time is what you haven't got.

Better sit down and have a cup of coffee while you try to figure out all those phone bills you now get at the end of each month. (Remember the good old days of one phone, one bill?) Will that coffee be decaf or regular; instant, drip or perk; flavored or plain? More decisions. Being a consumer has become a full-time job.

Maintaining the coffee-maker, the telephone and all the other time-saving gadgets takes time, too. When the phone stops working, for example, you can:

- Figure out whether your phone company plans to fix it. (Skip this step. They won't. It's always your fault.)
- Try to take the thing apart and figure out why it doesn't work.
- Spend twenty minutes sorting through 417 instruction manuals to try to find the one that came with the phone. (You can probably skip that step, too. The one manual you need is the one you didn't keep. See how much time I'm saving you already?)
- Call someone in to take a look—but you'd better plan on spending the day at home waiting for the repairer to show up.
- Take it to the store and try to get help there.
- Throw it away and buy a new one, which involves a trip to the mall.

After a few modern miracle appliances break, you learn to skip right to the last step, since most consumer items are made to be used and thrown away these days, and it often costs more to repair an appliance than to buy a new one. We live in a throw-away society.

Look how much trouble that innocent little telephone has caused you — and all this before it even rings, thereby disrupting your peace and concentration with a digitally recorded, computer-generated solicitation for the Save the Democrats and Other Endangered Species Fund.

And that's not all. Add to the phone frenzy the microwave mess, the hair-dryer hassle, the VCR vexation (does anybody over age twelve really understand how to program the thing to record two shows, two days apart?), the Cuisinart crush. . . .

Add to all these sad facts of modern life the even bleaker fact that it now takes two people bringing home paychecks to enable most families to get by, much less afford these gadgets and their inevitable replacements. The balance sheet shows a marked deficit in the "time saved" column.

We run ever faster and keep slipping behind

We've brought technology into the workplace too, of course, where computers, calculators and copiers that print on both sides, sort, collate and staple have allegedly increased our capacity to do more and better work. But we don't work shorter; we've simply increased our expectations of how much we should be able to accomplish in a day. As our "to-do" list keeps growing, we work longer and longer and still slip further behind. If by some miracle we actually check off every item, we're too exhausted to feel any satisfaction. We get up the next morning and make a new list.

After working deadly long hours and enduring our hectic schedules, we bring more work home with us. IBM couldn't sell personal computers when they advertised all the fun we'd have playing with them. But as soon as they told us we'd be able to "take work home on your little finger" with a floppy disk, PCs flew out of the stores.

No wonder so many of us resent our jobs and ruin Sunday by dreading Monday. TGIF could replace "In God we trust" as our national motto.

Are we really working more, or does it just seem that way?

In the late 1800s, the sixty-hour work week was the norm. By 1910, that figure had dropped to fifty-one hours, and in 1929, as the stock market got ready to take its famous swan dive, the average American put in forty-four hours per week. We bottomed out at about thirty-nine hours per week in the early 1970s, and folks were announcing the impending arrival of the Age of Leisure.

But something strange happened on our way to the perpetual vacation. We stopped working shorter and started working longer again. Now the average worker puts in about 164 extra hours of paid labor every year—that's a month more work. The percentage of workers spending more than forty-eight hours a week on the job has increased from 13 percent of the work force in 1948 to more than 20 percent in 1965, according to one survey.

The time-management clock-racers tell us to control that work time, to make more lists, to get rid of "time wasters" (people who want to sit down and chat for longer than thirty seconds), to screen out unimportant calls, and to hang up on those who somehow wriggle through the screen. Do we really have to become unbearably rude to survive in the work place?

Those time-crazed Type-A's career from one crisis to the next, seeming to get a lot of work done. But Type-A's tend to develop heart disease, ulcers and sleep disorders at an alarmingly high rate, and new studies indicate that they are actually less, not more, productive than their more laid-back Type-B colleagues. By bringing a frenzied sense of urgency to every encounter, they create stress—for themselves and those around them. And stress cripples and kills, corrupting mind, body and spirit.

The down side of the desktop publishing revolution

Your home and your work place probably have at least one thing in common: They're probably both overflowing with paper.

We are in the midst of the second great publishing revolution. Gutenberg and his movable type triggered the first one, bringing books out of the monastery and into the hands of the masses. The Macintosh computer has sparked the second wave of publishing populism, making everyone a potential publisher. You don't need to own the press, and you don't have to buy ink by the barrel. All you need is access to the magic box and a laser printer.

That's the good news: You, too, can be a publisher. The bad news is, so can everybody else. As a consequence, we're drowning in a flood of books, newsletters, newspapers, pamphlets, brochures, fliers and bumper stickers.

I read three daily newspapers, a dozen weeklies and perhaps eight to ten magazines a week. I skim, scan and/or read two hundred books a year. Since I teach a workshop on newsletters, I read and evaluate several hundred of them each year. I'm here to tell you that every interest group now has its own publication. If you don't believe me, grab a copy of *Writer's Market* and take a look. You'll find, among others:

- *The Mayberry Gazette*, the world authority on Mayberry, North Carolina (setting for "The Andy Griffith Show," as if you didn't know)
- *Lefthander Magazine*, circulation 26,000 — but no magazine yet for those of us who are ambidextrous
- *Massage Magazine*, "keeping those who touch in touch"
- *Shuttle, Spindle and Dyepot*, from the good folks at the Handweavers Guild of America
- *One Shot*, containing information about rock 'n' rollers who only had one hit record
- *The Pumper*, for folks in the liquid waste hauling industry — and more than that you don't want to know

One of my absolute favorites is *The Proper Mustard*, "The official newsletter of the Mount Horeb, Wisconsin, Mustard Museum."

You invite this stuff into your home. You even pay for it. But there's so much of it, you don't have time to read it all. So you graze, hoping to come upon something interesting or useful. Your primary goal is to turn the pages, to get to the end, to check it off the to-do list and get on to the next item. You're like a window shopper at the mall, walking down the center of a double-row of stores, glancing at the displays, until something entices you to stop and linger a few moments before hurrying on.

And those are the publications you *ask* for. You also get a flood of stuff you didn't ask for — the catalogs and "magalogs," the direct-mail market solicitations (that's the official term for "junk mail"), the brochures and the tear-stained letters, folded over once, that say "Open only if you've decided not to buy" and that begin, "Frankly, I don't understand."

You learn to fend the stuff off, so the pitch becomes more shrill. "You may have already won $1,000,000,000!!!!" one envelope screams. "Open this or we will kill your firstborn child!!!!!" the next one shrieks.

The moment you respond to one of the pitches, they sell your name to fifty more marketers, and the flood of mail swells higher. You just get yesterday's take sorted and stacked, tossing as much of it into the wastebasket unopened as you can, and here comes today's torrent. Only Sundays and holidays stem the flood.

No wonder you struggle to manage your time. Everybody wants a chunk of it.

Instant entertainment isn't fast enough

Even when we seek a little fun and relaxation, we don't stop speeding. We perch in front of our VCRs, remote controls clutched in our fists, and fast forward through the slow spots, zap the commercials, graze from station to station. If the story doesn't grab us — right now — we flee to another. "Entertain us!" we demand. And be quick about it. And so the entertainers, frantic to keep our attention, pack the first few seconds of every look-alike program with car chases, assaults and shock lines.

The VCR has given us the illusion of control over our entertainment environment. After all, we can now record a movie or program (if we can figure out the instructions, that is) and watch it whenever we want. But there are always new programs to record, and somehow we never get the time to watch the ones we've already recorded.

News in bits, briefs and bites

News has become another entertainment, another hurry-up symptom of our speed sickness. Television news programs shun "talking heads" and ideas in favor of vivid images of the daily disaster. Anchors engage in happy banter between lurid tales of rape and murder (do you truly want or need to know which body parts the mass-murderer allegedly ate?) and images of fire and flood. Reporters for the electronic media reduce every significant utterance to a seven-second "sound bite."

Newspapers and magazines break stories into bits and briefs, sidebars and digests, all based on the self-fulfilling prophecy of the reader's short attention span. Print screams for our attention with boxes and screens, color and pull quotes, holograms and scratch-and-sniff.

Trash journalism, whether in tabloid newspapers or on radio and television, has become an unspeakable assault on our humanity, an outrage to intelligence and honest emotion. But the lines between sleaze and the evening news, between the *National Enquirer* and *Esquire*, have faded and may soon disappear. The tabloid reports the politician's alleged affair; the "respectable" press then reports on the report.

Life as a two-minute drill

The jerky, violent rhythms of football have replaced the slower, gentler unfolding of baseball as our national game, even as our lives have become a series of two-minute drills. And watching the 49ers or Redskins is the only exercise many of us get. We buy the membership to the club, the home gym equipment or the exercycle, but we never seem to find the time to use it. We know we *should* exercise — just as we know we should eat oat bran — but knowing and doing are two very different things.

We eat so fast, we hardly notice what we're eating — which may explain in part why we eat so much of the wrong stuff — or even how much of it we've eaten. By the time our stomachs can get the signal back to our mouths to cease stuffing, we've consumed well beyond need or even satiation.

Breaking the back of the book

Relatively few of us read books. The number of sales needed to propel a book to the top of the *New York Times* best-seller lists (positions occupied, as I write these words, by *Scarlett*, a sequel to *Gone With the Wind*, in fiction; *Me*, the autobiography of a movie star, in nonfiction; and *Final Exit*, a book on how to commit suicide, on the "self-help" list) would produce a television rating of less than one point, not even a blip on the Nielsen ratings. (It usually takes about twenty points, or twenty million television sets, to keep a show on the networks.)

Books are too slow, and they're too much work. We have easier ways to get information and to have our stories told to us.

Speed-reading courses teach us how to paw the pages, gathering key words and "shaking" meaning loose at 5,000 words per minute. When you first pick up a book in a speed-reading class, your instructor tells you to break its spine, so the pages will turn faster. To me that feels like breaking your dog's spine before you begin his obedience lesson, so that he will be more tractable.

Nature by the numbers

Nature itself has become too slow for us. Instead of taking the time and effort to seek it out, we capture and compress it on television and juice it up with time-lapse photography. The flower thrusts up from the ground, the bud emerges, ripens, bursts into bloom—all in a few seconds, while the narrator explains the meaning of the mystery. Break for commercial.

Nature's not like that, of course. Flowers unfold gently, imperceptibly. You have to be there, to put in the time, if you want to feel the miracle. Perhaps we're so quick to destroy our earth because we no longer take the time to experience it.

Mismanaging time

We are the generation after instant gratification. Instant isn't fast enough anymore, and we don't seem to be feeling gratified.

We take seminars and listen to tapes to learn how to "manage" time, which we equate with money.

We awaken to an alarm, strap a watch to our wrists and spend the rest of the day trying to keep to a schedule—our own if we're lucky, somebody else's if we're not. Even our leisure activities become another series of scheduled obligations on a checklist.

We construct tight schedules for our kids, too. After locking them in school all day, we speed them from piano recital to soccer match to French lesson. We don't see much of them, of course, but when we do, we make sure it's "quality time" (perhaps the most cruel hoax of our age), thereby putting such a massive strain on our few shared moments they collapse under the weight of tension and fatigue.

Listening to the clock instead of the muse

And what of our need for creative expression, that divine drive to make new ideas and images, to tell new stories and to tell the old stories in new ways? Instead of listening to the inner voice of inspiration, we hear the ticking of the clock. Every second we aren't doing something "useful" or "important" or "productive" moves us one second closer to the time when we must go on to the next activity on the schedule. And what will we have to show for it? How will we prove our worth, earn our place?

We call the resultant time-paralysis a creative "block," but it's really just another symptom of our speed sickness. In becoming ever more time-conscious, we lose the ability to lose ourselves in our projects. Awareness of time, after all, is just another kind of self-consciousness, another layer separating us from our true work and our heart's pleasure. When we become trapped in time, we become less productive, less creative, less alive.

We're not living for this moment. We're living for the next one, for some future horizon that recedes faster and faster the faster we try to catch up with it.

Ask any ten people you meet how they're doing, and nine will respond "busy." It's the national disease.

And at the end of another frantic day, when it should be time at last to lay our burdens down, we even shave time off of sleep and try to manage and regulate our slumber, with the result that 80 percent of us, according to some estimates, are chronically sleep-deprived—and thus chronically grouchy and inattentive.

This is crazy. The carousel's running wild. Nobody's at the controls. Life is whizzing by in a blur. It's making us sick.

We've got to get off that carousel.

Getting better and better at measuring less and less

It wasn't always this way, of course. Once upon a time, a long time ago, there was no time. In fact, for most of our existence, we had no clocks or calendars, no way to measure the passage of our lives except to note the movements of the sun, the moon and the stars, the rhythms of our bodies, the ebb and flow of the seasons. We ate when we were hungry, slept when it got dark, got up when it got light again.

About 4000 B.C., cave dwellers began making notches on bones to mark the waxings and wanings of the moon. From that point on, we've created more sophisticated and precise ways to measure time, which we came to see as tangible and, in most Western cultures, linear — a time line rather than a time circle or time ripples on a pond.

Some of our best thinkers have tried to remind us that past-present-future is only one way of understanding time, not necessarily the "right" one. Einstein demonstrated that measurements of time are actually fluid and subjective. Novelist Kurt Vonnegut Jr. invented a race of aliens called Tralfamadorians, who could see the entire stretch of time at once, the way we might stand back and view a mural.

But most of us remain stuck on a linear time line. And in learning to live by the clock, we've learned to ignore the rhythms of the body and the earth. Unlike our forebears, who ate when they were hungry and slept when the sun went down, we eat when our culture says it's time to eat and sleep when the clock tells us we should. Perhaps we can trace our willful abuses of our bodies to this critical aspect of our cultural evolution.

Our ability to measure the time we had invented and imposed on reality is now incredibly precise. By the late 1960s we had developed a cesium clock accurate to one second every 3,000 years or one-millionth of a second per day. But who in the name of Copernicus could possibly need to know the time accurate to one-millionth of a second?

Exploring your personal sense of time

What would happen to your sense of time if you threw out all the time-keepers? You've no doubt done so on occasion, becoming so absorbed in what you're doing that you lost all track of time. Such times usually carry price tags. You may miss an appointment, stay up too late, fail to get your work done. But even so, you probably associate such "timeless" times with strong feelings of pleasure and well-being.

Think of a few such times you've experienced. How do you feel about these experiences now? Can you imagine a whole day during which you took no note of time? What would you learn about yourself and your relationship with time if you actually lived such a day?

Your initial ℞ for recovering from speed sickness

If you should survive to age seventy, experts tell us, you'll probably wind up spending:

- six months waiting at stop lights
- at least that long in the express lane at the supermarket, behind the guy who has thirteen items and pays with pennies
- two years on the telephone, most of it on hold or talking to a recording device
- three years being sick
- six years eating
- nineteen years working
- twenty-three years sleeping

Want to change anything about the way you spend your time? Here are a few suggestions to consider.

You can change just about anything about the way you live each day

A lot of what you consider natural reactions to circumstances turn out to be learned behavior, reinforced through repetition until they become habits and take on the aspect of natural law or moral imperative. If you want to change the way you respond, you can do it.

You must work at it

The longer you reinforce your habit responses, the harder they may be to alter or erase and replace. You'll need to catch yourself before you react, so you can replace the pattern response with a new, more useful, more liberating reaction.

You must commit yourself to the effort

If you simply stand at the base of the mountain and wish you could be at the top, no matter how ardently you wish or how positively you think, you'll never get off the canyon floor. You must commit yourself to the climb, and you must be willing to pay the price in terms of time, effort and the loss of all the things you can't do while you're climbing the mountain.

You must believe that you will be successful

Not "I hope I can" or "I'll try hard" but "I *will*." The more times you succeed, the easier it will be to believe in the next success. Take note of and enjoy all your triumphs, no matter how small. Appreciate yourself for the effort you make and the changes you create.

You must take total responsibility for the outcome

No matter how well you train and how much you learn, a sudden storm could come up and wipe you off the face of that mountain you want so much to climb. But you must act as if only your actions matter and you are completely responsible for the outcome.

If you commit yourself totally to climbing the mountain, you still might not succeed. But if you don't commit yourself to the climb, you're certain to fail. And even if you never reach the top of the mountain, you'll find your life's meaning and your soul's delight in the commitment and the climb.

You must do it your way

Study my suggestions and those of others. Then discover your own strategy.

Your methods for easing yourself out of time and compulsion and into freedom and choice may include prayer, meditation and visualization. You may modify these methods. And you may come up with a method the rest of us don't even have a name for yet. (If you do, write a book. I'll read it.) You must invent your own rules, based on an honest monitoring of your progress to see if what you're doing really works.

You must spend the time

A woman ten years out of college was considering going to law school.

"But if I do go to law school," she lamented to a friend, "I'll be forty-two years old by the time I graduate."

"And how old will you be," the wise friend countered, "if you don't go to law school?"

Anything of real worth or importance takes time. You may have fallen in love at first glance, but building a relationship takes a lifetime. The impulse to lose forty pounds, write a novel or climb a mountain may come in an instant. But crash diets don't work, there are no instantaneous novels, and there's no short way up the mountain. Carrying out your intention and your commitment takes time.

That's what this book is all about—taking the time to reclaim your life.

Owning it

Naming your own brand of speed sickness

Before you can begin to solve a problem, you must know what it is.

Is "speed sickness" the right name for what ails you? Is a virus the right metaphor for you? If not, give your problem a more appropriate name.

Speed sickness comes in many varieties and produces many symptoms. Take a few minutes to list the symptoms you see in yourself.

When did each symptom on your list begin to develop? Try to trace the symptom to its origin. When did you notice the tension in your shoulders, the temper flare-ups, the feeling of frustration and futility at the end of each day?

Which factors in your life accompanied the onset of each symptom? Did specific changes—new job, lack of money, problems in a relationship, new obligations—trigger the symptom? We can't always know how or to what we react. We're complex critters. But only you can begin to understand your reactions.

Such self-analysis is worth the effort—and yes, the time—it takes. The more you can name and understand your situation, the more you'll benefit from our explorations in this book—and the more you'll be able to develop your own solutions as we consider possibilities for reclaiming your life.

CHAPTER TWO

Can you really manage time?

"We never shall have any more time.
We have, and we have always had, all
the time there is."
ARNOLD BENNETT, *HOW TO LIVE ON 24 HOURS A DAY*

Learning when to control and when to let go

A Delevan, Wisconsin, twelve-year-old recently won the Madison Symphony Orchestra audition and, with it, the right to perform at two youth concerts. According to the story in the paper, this extraordinary young man practices his violin for two hours a day and works out with the piano for another thirty minutes. He's into photography and herpetology (I think that means he likes lizards), writes fiction and poetry, and takes tennis lessons. All this on top of the usual demands of school and the pressures of being an emerging adolescent. Just your typical preteen overachiever.

Does he *like* doing all that? The story didn't say. Does he ever have time to just goof off and be a kid? I sure hope so. If he doesn't, he could go from twelve-year-old superstar to thirteen-year-old burnout.

Portrait of a clock-racer

Let's call him Rapid Ron, the perpetual-motion man, the very model of an efficient time manager.

RR bounds out of bed at precisely 5:22 A.M. and does twelve minutes of deep-knee bends and sit-ups while chanting his time mantra: "I can't control time. But I *can* control *me!*"

He takes a cold shower while listening to a tape of Robert Bly's *Iron John* that has been "compressed" to leave out the gaps, thus giving Ron 8.6 minutes of tape for every 5.3 minutes of shower. He scans the business briefs in the newspaper over instant breakfast and coffee, shaves and handles three calls on the car phone on the way to the office.

By leaving the house no later than 6:27 and holding his speed at a constant 57 m.p.h., he can hit every green light on the way downtown (assuming that he's able to weave through or scare off the slowpokes who insist on going the speed limit).

While his secretary screens all irrelevant calls, he dictates drafts of memos, letters and work orders into his portable cassette recorder while moving from one tightly scheduled appointment to the next, including a meeting over lunch.

Home again, he shares dinner and eighteen minutes of quality time with the family (except that Ron Jr. is at soccer practice, and Veronica is up in her room moping). He then retires to the den to watch a previously taped football game on the VCR, fast-forwarding through the huddles, the commercials and John Madden's commentary, so that he finishes the game in just under fourteen minutes. He turns the sound off on the game and plays subliminal motivational messages.

He skims, scans, shakes and paws his way through a stack of business correspondence and professional reading, checks the last item off the "Priority-A" to-do list, drafts tomorrow's list, and tumbles into bed at 11:22, right after the local weather forecast, for six hours of sleep, the minimum he can get by on. Ron has had a little trouble falling asleep lately (can't imagine why), so he takes a sleeping tablet, to be sure not to waste precious time tossing and turning.

Life is not all work for Ron, of course. He schedules lots of time for fun. There's his 6:15 A.M. tee-time on Saturday morning—an early start means less waiting for the duffers and hackers, and Ron hates to wait. Saturday afternoon from 2:00 to 4:00 is reserved for "family fun"—although as the kids have reached their teens, family fun has increasingly meant Ron and wife Rhonda going to the movies. They throw a party every other Saturday night—they can take care of a slew of social obligations at once that way. And of course there are special events, like the drafting of the family Christmas letter, which takes care of the personal correspondence for the year.

Does all this sound a bit extreme? I hope so. In fact, I hope it sounds downright crazy. Our hypothetical clock-racer is controlling himself to death. By racing through the day, he's winding himself up and wearing himself out, setting himself up for heart disease, high blood pressure and chronic sleep disorders. He's also lowering rather than raising his efficiency at work. Worse yet, by racing through life at warp speed, Ron distances himself from family and friends and from his own internal stirrings and whimsies.

And he's probably not having much fun in the process.

No time for loving?

Ron and Rhonda may even have sex less often than they used to. Who has time? Or energy? Consider the great New York City blackout of November 1965 or the great Chicago snowstorm of January 1967. In both instances, the cities experienced a huge increase in the birth rate nine months later. Perhaps it was the romance of candlelight and fireplaces. But perhaps, too, a lot of folks made love because all the distractions had been stripped away, at least for one night, and there was time for each other.

Those intimate moments may be getting shorter as well as less frequent. When lovemaking becomes just another item on the schedule instead of a spontaneous pleasure and an act of mutual love, leisurely seduction vanishes. Maybe the "sexual liberation" of the 1960s was really the first great time-management technique, eliminating time-consuming preliminaries such as dating, courtship and learning your partner's full name.

Asking "Lakein's Question"

Books purporting to tell us how to live more time-efficient lives date back at least to 1910 and Arnold Bennett's *How to Live on 24 Hours a Day*. But the time-management movement began in earnest in the early 1970s — about the time the work week was starting to lengthen — with a barrage of self-help books, seminars and tapes. Perhaps in part clock-racing began as a backlash against the laid-back, go-with-the-flow ethic of the 1960s. Perhaps it grew out of our sensing that we lacked control over our lives. The tightening economy, the two wage-earner family, and the need for moonlighting to make ends meet have probably all contributed.

Whatever the cause, the time was right in 1973 for Alan Lakein to give the movement its classic text, *How to Get Control of Your Time & Your Life*. We must "work smarter, not harder," Lakein told us. And then he spent several hundred pages telling us how.

You can "drift, drown or decide," Lakein warned. You need to exert control over your time, which is to say your life, by planning. Make a daily to-do list. Establish A, B and C priorities. Then rank the A items, tackling the "A-1" essential items first.

Use commute, coffee break, lunch and waiting times productively.

Don't sleep your life away. Handle paper once. Screen out the irrelevant. Say "no" to the time-wasters.

Above all, constantly ask yourself the "Lakein question" — "What's the best use of my time right now?"

Lakein warned against becoming a compulsive overorganizer, an overdoer, a "time nut." He advised us to allow for flexibility by scheduling slack time, to deal with the unexpected. He also advocated free time. Relaxing, he maintained, is a good use of time, and sometimes you can get more done by doing nothing.

But many ignored this wisdom. While Lakein went on to advise everybody from AT&T executives to Gloria Steinem, other gurus of the clock-racer movement rushed their own versions of the gospel into print, without the warnings about becoming obsessive and with detailed timelogs to fill out for each moment of your life.

A few, like Tony and Robbie Fanning in their book *Get It All Done & Still Be Human*, set as the goal feeling good rather than doing more. But most of the clock-racer books and tapes that followed Lakein stressed packing every minute of every day with as much productive activity as possible. Self-discipline, surely the second most abused notion in our culture (after "quality time"), would enable us to take control of our lives, the clock-racers assured us. So we armed ourselves with cellular telephones, message machines, beepers, VCRs, fax machines and all those other devices allegedly created to help us save, compress, densify and otherwise work time to death. By the late 1980s, 2.5 million fax machines graced the planet, a million of them in the United States. And yet, most of us still feel no more in control of our lives than before. Instead we feel wrung out, strung out and stressed out.

What we *don't* feel is good.

We still have too much to do, and we don't feel satisfied with what we're doing. We're so busy, we don't even remember what we might like to do, if only we had the time. We schedule instead of live. Who has time to feel or think?

Six fundamental principles for passionate living

None of the truly productive people I know make Priority-A lists or keep time logs. They just do what they do, with a passion and zest that sometimes look like insanity. But they don't care what they look like to the rest of us. They just let it rip, 100 percent, holding nothing back.

If they stay up all night reading a book, it's because they want to know what's in it, not because they feel a compulsion to check it off a list. If they let the book sit unopened while they stare at the moonrise and the star shower, the book will just have to wait.

In the chapters that follow, we'll examine ways to modify your life, so that you live instead of schedule, enjoy instead of race. We'll adapt a few of the more helpful principles of clock-racing, taking a close look at potential time-wasters in your life. We'll talk about stress and worry and examine the roles of rest, sleep and exercise in a balanced, satisfying life. I'll invite you to take a new look at how you live your life.

For now, let's establish a foundation of basic principles—not of clock-racing, but of passionate, productive living.

The first principle, which surpasses all principles and can set you free: You get to decide how you spend your time.

You get to choose how much is enough and how good is good enough. You get to decide what is and what isn't a waste of time. If you make a schedule, the schedule exists to serve you, not the other way around. You get to decide when to follow and when to abandon your schedule.

Nobody has the right to demand, borrow or steal your time. You of course freely surrender this right to loved ones and friends, who take precedence over anything you had planned. But you owe no such allegiance to the pushy acquaintance, the bored co-worker, the salesperson in search of a commission. If you deny them your time and attention, they may dislike you for it. But you needn't pay attention to these or any other judgments, unless you find them helpful.

Second fundamental principle: Telephones, faxes and beepers are tools, not forces of nature.

You get to decide whether to answer the telephone. It may be heresy to let a phone ring, but it is *not* a crime.

You get to decide whether to open the mail, respond to the fax, read the magazine, turn on the television, pay any attention to it once it's on, or throw it in the garbage.

Use the tools. Don't let them use you.

Third fundamental principle: Make possibilities, not plans.

Stay loose, flexible, open to the moment. Listen to your intuitions, your moods, your fancies. Know that the most important thing you'll do today may not be on your to-do list.

Just because you've done it before doesn't mean you must do it again. Just because you've never done it before doesn't mean you can't do it now. Look for new ways to reorganize and unorganize your day.

Fourth fundamental principle: Give yourself a break.

According to the old story, if you put a frog in a pot of water on the stove and turn the heat up slowly, you can boil the poor frog before it figures out what's going on.

Have you been gradually turning up the heat in your life and adjusting to rising stress levels? You may tell yourself that you work better under pressure, but it isn't true. You've just gotten used to the heat.

Give yourself enough lead time to do a good job and still enjoy your life. Don't time that dash downtown so that you must hit every green light and find a parking space right in front of the office to be on time for your appointment. Leave early. If you get stuck in traffic, welcome the wait as an opportunity to breathe deeply, daydream, meditate or people-watch.

Be gentle with yourself. Treat yourself at least as well as you'd treat the family dog.

Before you race off to the next task, reward yourself for work well done, for an onerous job finally finished.

Fifth fundamental principle: Whenever possible, put it off.

If you really don't want or need to do it right now, don't. Maybe you won't have to do it at all.

This principle obviously doesn't apply to filling out your income tax form, returning your rented video, or paying off your parking ticket. It doesn't apply to the promises you make to others. But I'll bet it does apply to at least half the memos, the solicitations, the banging, harping, pleading demands on your time that assault you every day.

I keep a paper compost heap in the middle of my desk. When I get a memo or letter I don't have to deal with right away, I toss it on the heap and let it decompose. By the time I uncover it, it's often too late to do anything about it. The world seems to keep right on turning anyway.

Sixth fundamental principle: Don't spend time, save time, or waste time. Live.

We'll spend the rest of this book exploring what that might mean for you.

Owning it

Developing your own fundamental principles

Did you find anything new among my "fundamental principles"? Do you agree or disagree strongly with anything you've just read? Let yourself respond to these ideas.

Make your own set of principles. You have a big advantage over me here. At some point, after all the rewriting and revision, all the scribbled notes on little slips of paper stuffed in pockets, I had to send this stuff to the publishers and let them print it. Now I'm stuck with what I wrote. But you can write your fundamental principles in pencil, or with chalk on the sidewalk, or in the sand on the beach, and then change them as your perceptions deepen and your self-awareness grows. Don't be afraid to contradict yourself and to change your mind. And don't be afraid to let your thoughts change the way you live.

Hang on to this beginning list of principles. When we finish our explorations, I'll invite you to take another crack at creating your personal declaration of independence, your prescription for recovery from speed sickness.

CHAPTER THREE

Finding your own truth

*"To be nobody but yourself in a world
doing its best to make you everybody
else means to fight the hardest battle
any human can ever fight
and never stop fighting."*

e.e. cummings

Invasion of the time-snatchers

Perhaps you recall the classic chiller *Invasion of the Body Snatchers*
(I'm thinking of the original with Kevin McCarthy, rather than the re-
make with Donald Sutherland, but either version illustrates the point).
In this nightmare vision, as folks fall asleep, they become possessed by
alien pod creatures, who take over consciousness and volition. You can
tell folks have been podded by their glazed expressions and halting
speech.

This movie did for taking a nap what *Psycho* did for taking a shower.

For me, the scariest part is the way the pods capture their prey —
not through open confrontation and combat, but through the subject's
passive surrender of will.

I don't want to be an alarmist, but if you look around the mall on
any Saturday afternoon (something I try never to do), you'll encounter
a lot of hollow looks. Have the body snatchers been at work in your
town? If folks look and behave like zombies while out supposedly having
fun ("malling" has become a recreational verb), imagine how they must
look on Monday morning.

The greatest time-waster of all—trying to be somebody else

You can try to save time by doing exactly what you're doing now, only doing it more efficiently. If you get organized, make a list, prioritize your tasks, manage the flow of paper, you *can* save some time.

You may have given away a lot of the control over your day-to-day activities. If so, this sort of traditional time-management approach can help you, as long as all that list-making and prioritizing don't wind up taking more time than they save. We'll spend a couple of chapters developing ways to eliminate your time-wasters.

But reclaiming your life may involve a more fundamental change in the way you choose to live. Rather than beginning by fine-tuning life as you now live it, let's first look at some underlying assumptions about that life.

Two great time-snatchers are on the loose, and unless you keep eternally vigilant, they may compromise your ability to spend your time—which is to say your life—doing what you want to do with zest and enthusiasm.

Worry is one of the two major time-snatchers. The time you spend worrying accomplishes nothing and robs you of energy, vitality and will. We'll tackle that worthy foe in the next chapter.

In this chapter we'll focus on the other great absorber of time and energy: *the creation and maintenance of a persona or public self*.

The three faces of Eve—and of the rest of us

Therapist Mary Edwards specializes in the treatment of people with multiple personality disorders. These folks have separate selves or personalities, sometimes dozens of them, Edwards says, all inhabiting the same body but most unaware of the existence of the others. The split usually begins in early childhood, the result of some trauma too horrible for the conscious mind to handle. In the popular movie *The Three Faces of Eve*, the trauma occurs when a child's parents force her to kiss her dead grandmother good-bye. Through therapy, the adult child is later able to dredge up the suppressed memory and, ultimately, to accept and integrate her three "selves."

People with MPD tend to be quite creative and even gifted, Edwards says. "They're way ahead of us," she says. "They have much to teach us." And, she says, we're a lot more like them than we may realize.

Edwards and other experts distinguish between "pathological multiplicity" (folks recognized as having multiple personality disorder) and "normal multiplicity" (the rest of us). We are, Edwards says, not one personality but three: the one we're aware of, the one we're not aware of, and the observer. The two unconscious personalities "are there to protect us," she says. They have "an awareness all their own" that surfaces in dreams.

If the conscious, controlling self (we've learned to call it the ego) feels strong and secure, it will allow those subpersonalities to express themselves relatively freely, Edwards says. But if it feels threatened, it will suppress characteristics that don't conform to its sense of proper behavior and may then project those characteristics onto other people.

By suppressing so much of our true selves, Edwards says, most of us use only a small percentage of our talents and creativity, express only a fraction of our desires, miss experiencing much of our potential for joy. We'd be better off, she says, if we learned to name, embrace and experience our other selves.

Change your hair, change your life

Back in the 1950s, only 7 percent of American women would admit to dying their hair. Such activity carried connotations of promiscuity. A product named Clairol and an advertising executive named Shirley Polykoff changed all that with the immortal line, "Does she or doesn't she? Only her hairdresser knows for sure."

Clairol followed that campaign with the equally famous "Is it true blondes have more fun?" Evidently, a lot of brunettes and redheads figured it was worth a try. Sales of hair dyes, rinses and tints soared, and Clairol claimed a dominant share of the market.

The ad didn't ask "Is it true that you would have more fun if you had blonde hair?" It suggested instead a more fundamental change, calling on un-blondes to be something other than what they were to enjoy life more fully.

What sort of man reads *Playboy*?

Another advertising campaign from the 1950s attempted to educate young American males in the fine art of living the good life. "What kind of man reads *Playboy*?" the ads challenged. The *Playboy* Man (read "cool," "sophisticated" and "wildly successful with women") buys the right stereo, car, clothing and alcohol. You are what you buy, these and many other ads seemed to suggest.

Creating an acceptable self

Whether or not you remember these antique ads, I'll bet you got the message. Parents, teachers, friends and media images taught you acceptable and unacceptable ways to look, act and believe. You learned which behaviors earned you approval, which "self" of all your possible selves would be accepted and loved. Using this knowledge, you constructed an acceptable personality and internalized the rules of conformity.

You can suppress traits that don't conform—dangerous thoughts, naughty impulses—but you can't destroy them. They go into hiding, creating subconscious personalities or shadow selves, the cast of characters for your dreams and a rich source of insight into human nature for anyone willing to venture into wild, uncharted areas of the psyche.

Your public persona might earn the acceptance and love you want. But you lose a lot, too—all those possible other selves you might have been, the authentic impulses you never express, the creative resources that might have enabled you to live more fully, effectively and joyfully.

And your mind may pick up a constant, numbing fear: If you must suppress some of your impulses and inclinations, they must be wrong or even evil. That means *you* must be wrong or evil, too. You may fool the world into thinking you're okay, the reasoning goes, but deep inside, you know what a wretch you really are. You may become terrified that a shadow self will emerge at the wrong time, like a belch at the dinner table, and you'll be found out for the faker you know yourself to be. When that happens, all your love and acceptance will be snatched away, leaving you alone and miserable.

Only in moments of extreme intimacy do you ever get to see anybody else's shadow selves. Usually you see only the assured, confident masks others wear. So you may believe you're the only pretender, all alone in your deception and fear, the only one in the world who must forever wear the lying mask.

It takes a lot of energy to create the mask and to keep it from slipping. The constant anxiety and underlying sorrow costs still more. The strain may even make you sick.

"You are healthy when you are most yourself," according to Dr. Kenneth Pelletier, an expert on links between stress and disease. "There is no prescription for health other than that. Do anything that gives you a sense of enthusiasm and joy, and be yourself."

If you could put down your mask, release your fear, welcome your shadow selves out into the sunlight—imagine the energy, health and joy you might also release.

It's easy to say but terribly hard to do, after a lifetime of keeping the mask firmly in place. It may be the hardest work you'll ever do—and the most rewarding.

Here's a profile of one who refused to wear the mask. His story may help you to begin lowering your own mask.

Meet "America's most dangerous community journalist"

Norbert Blei grew up in Chicago and came to love the City with the Broad Shoulders, with its ethnic neighborhoods, elevated trains and, most of all, that concoction of bun, weiner and condiments known as the Chicago Dog. Blei flourished on Chicago Dogs and chaos, creating a life as an experimental novelist (he called his first novel *Second Novel*) and journalist (he worked for his hero, columnist Mike Royko, at the City News Bureau). He taught a little high school English, freelanced, survived.

Blei figured the living would be considerably less expensive out on the fringe, making it easier to support himself doing what he wanted to do, so he moved from Chicago to rural Ellison Bay in Wisconsin's scenic Door County in 1969. With long, graying hair and sweeping walrus mustache, he looked the part of the rural eccentric. His writing studio—a converted chicken coop—enhanced the image. But Blei wasn't trying to create an image. He was creating a life, piecing together enough paying work to live while claiming the rest of his time for living.

Blei hired on as a columnist for the *Door County Reminder*, a local shopper. Shoppers don't usually hire columnists—especially not a columnist with national publications to his credit—and writers with emerging national reputations don't usually write for shoppers. But publisher Lon Kopitzke wanted folks to notice his shopper, so he agreed to run Blei's pieces without censoring them.

Blei had some things he wanted to say, and for four frantic months, he said them in the *Reminder*.

Folks noticed.

"Blei/AT LARGE" immediately took on the rival *Door County Advocate* (or "Aggravate," as Blei called it) and its "Blubonic box plague." Blei claimed that the *Advocate*'s plastic newspaper holders affixed to posts were a blight on the landscape. Blei ultimately won that battle.

Blei also took on nearby Green Bay, which he called "Grey Bay," equating a visit there with a death sentence. He suggested that the once-feared Green Bay Packers be renamed the "Green Bay Turkeys."

He called down to his subconscious cast of characters to create a secretary named "Lovta Du More X," an ex-hooker, ex-porn star and ex-born again and again Christian. He let Lovta answer the "male" and dispense advice. Local fundamentalists were not amused.

Nor were local business owners thrilled when Blei issued what was to have been the first of a multipart blueprint for Door County's future. He advocated "slamming the damn Door" on Illinois tourists and on all development. He urged residents to tear up the roads and let the peninsula revert to its natural state.

Door County, population 26,500, entertains some 750,000 tourists per summer. The visitors bring traffic and confusion, yes, but they leave behind about $120 million. Local merchants were less than eager to slam any doors on them.

Advertisers began putting pressure on publisher Kopitzke (whom Blei referred to as "Lonnie Let's Chat," after the name of Kopitzke's weekly column) to bounce Blei. Several threatened to pull their ads, a shopper's sole source of revenue.

Kopitzke hung semitough. He submitted the matter to a referendum of the readers, and Blei came out on the short end of a 221-171 vote. Despite the fact that more than two hundred letters later poured in passionately supporting Blei, Kopitzke fired his controversial columnist. He allowed Blei one final, massive farewell, a twenty-five-page opus supposedly recounting a conversation between Blei and Lovta at the local A.C. Tap.

Blei went underground, later resurfacing to write a new column, this time in the persona of the Coyote, a creature, Blei wrote, who would never "mistake cowardice for reasonableness."

That's as far as the saga goes. Blei is busy living the next installment.

Letting the self emerge

Blei is Blei. You are you, unique and uniquely gifted. The world needs the authentic you, being all of yourself and nobody else.

"This is my way," the philosopher Nietzsche wrote. "What is your way? *The* way doesn't exist."

But how do you begin to create that authentic "you" as opposed to a masked self? You don't. The real you is already there. You need only let it emerge.

Take off the mask. Stop pretending. Be what you are.

Set your own standards. Strip your life of any object or action that is false to your true self, that clutters and complicates your life and separates you from your true impulses.

It won't be easy, especially at first. The longer you've responded as your masked self, the more automatic those responses have become. Your first thought will be the one you were taught to have. Your first impulse will be the acceptable impulse, the "right" behavior, the desire you've learned to let yourself have.

Take a deep breath, challenge that first response, and ask yourself if that's what you really want to do. If your guts tell you that what you were about to do is false to what you believe, don't do it.

If others disapprove or fail to understand—as they surely will—grant them the freedom to react as they must. You want their love and approval, of course. But you don't *need* it. And when you drop the mask, you'll begin to attract those who can approve of and love you for what you are, not for what you've worked so hard to seem to be.

"Somewhere along the line of development," Eleanor Roosevelt wrote at age fifty-seven, "we discover what we really are, and then we make our real decision, for which we are responsible. Make that decision primarily for yourself, because you can never really live anyone else's life."

Learning to climb the mountain because you're there

When her husband got a job offer out in Seattle, my colleague and friend Lindy Bruce had to pull up her Madison, Wisconsin, roots, leave friends and job behind, and head west. Her letters were full of news of the search for a new house, new job, new purpose. Underneath the optimism, I read sadness and loneliness. Lindy's a dog lover, and when her beloved Strider died, she hit bottom.

"I realized I had nothing to lose," she told me on a recent visit back to Madison. "So I decided to just do whatever I wanted."

She realized she didn't need to be around people and to be accepted by them all the time. Being alone was okay, too. And she didn't need to have a job to have value.

She got a new dog, intensified her aerobic exercise program, lost fifteen pounds, got a new hairdo, and started climbing mountains voraciously. Dangling from a rope out on some absurdly steep slope, she learned that you don't climb mountains a little bit, and you don't hope yourself to the top. You must bring your entire self to the climb, and you must burn with the conviction that you'll make it.

Lindy radiates energy, vitality and confidence. She has claimed her life. She is finding her way.

Seeking your own truth

"It ain't what we don't know that gets us into trouble," Will Rogers once observed. "It's what we know for sure that ain't so."

Everybody knew that eggs, butter, cheese and milk constituted a healthy breakfast. Now everybody knows that dairy products are agents of slow death and that oat bran and prunes are the way to nutritional and spiritual well-being.

Everybody knew that God placed our flat planet in the exact center of the universe. Now we know that earth is but a tiny, tangential blip in the vast expanse.

Everybody knew that our forests would last forever, that we could never pollute all our waters or exhaust all our land. Today we know that we live in a closed ecosystem of finite resources. Tomorrow we will encounter the age of scarcity.

In the 1950s, we knew that a high-paying job, a house in the sub-urbs, and lots of expensive gadgets would make us happy. In the 1960s, we knew that dropping out and turning on led to peace and enlighten-ment. In the 1970s, we knew that the simple life of wood-burning stoves and homemade bread brought satisfaction. In the 1980s, we embraced fat stock portfolios.

What will be the new "truth"?

Folks will go on telling you how you must live to be happy. But nobody can tell you how to live. Today's cant is tomorrow's folly. What does your experience tell you? You'll find your truth only by keeping open to the lessons that your experience wants to teach you. Listen to others; then decide for yourself.

This advice, of course, applies to everything you read in this book. I'm no wiser than the rest, and I don't have your answers.

Don't be trapped by past decisions. Because you did it yesterday isn't a valid reason to do it today. Make your decision anew; it will be right for this moment. Tomorrow will require a new decision.

Learn again to listen to your inner impulses and inclinations. They'll tell you who you are and what you want to do. That doesn't mean you'll act on every impulse. Your actions have consequences, a price to pay, for yourself and for those around you. Often the price is too high, espe-cially when your actions would hurt those who love and rely on you. But accept and embrace the impulse, even if you must reject the action it seems to demand. Don't judge it as "bad." Don't judge it at all. Just let it be what it is and then let it go.

Listening to your impulses doesn't mean you'll behave like a selfish animal. Instead, your more selfless and generous impulses are likely to dominate as you create your own set of ethics.

Declaring peace

When you subdue and suppress your impulses, thoughts and desires, you wage war against yourself. As you create your acceptable self, you must immediately begin defending it against subversion from within.

Declare a cease-fire. Listen to the inner self. It may babble and howl at the moon at first. Be patient. After all, you've kept it bound and gagged in the basement for a long time. Gradually it will calm down and speak the truth.

You may also have been fiercely defending your masked self against outside threats, real and imagined, from those who want to judge or control you. You may resent the people close to you for seeming to force you to wear that mask. If so, you're spending a lot of time and energy trying to prove that your way is right, the other therefore wrong. The less certain you are, the harder you fight.

Lay down your arms. Surrender. Seek to be peaceful rather than right. Walk away from the endless battle that nobody ever wins. That war requires so much of your psychic energy; when you cease fighting, you'll experience an enormous peace dividend of energy, confidence and well-being.

Peace is more than the absence of war. It's the active pursuit of your path, the lustful singing of your song.

Owning it

Finding the power in the pause

You may have lost your true self in noise and motion, which create the illusion of progress. You won't discover your inner voice until you still the other voices inside and outside of you. Wait in the quiet for the inner voice to direct you.

You may have lost your true reaction in the automatic response, which gives the illusion of decisiveness. To stop killing your genuine impulses, catch yourself just before you pull the trigger. Slow down. Discover the power in the pause. Feel urgency and compulsion slip away. Feel the true self emerge and, with it, a flood of warmth and well-being.

By giving this time away, you'll receive time—not minutes of "saved" time each day, but your whole life, to live precisely as you please.

When you wake up, lay still for a few minutes. Quiet the yammering of the masked self. Remember your dreams or the feelings that enveloped you just before you broke through to wakefulness. Imagine your day—the decisions you'll make, the decisions others will try to make for you. Allow yourself to react and feel. Experience your power.

Select specific times during the day when you'll slow down to note how you feel about the decisions you make and the way you spend your time. Breathe deeply. Allow yourself to decide based on your feelings, hunches, intuitions.

Once a day, do something you ordinarily wouldn't do but would like to try. Eat falafel for lunch. Skip lunch and go for a brisk walk. Skip the walk and browse through a store you've never been in. Listen to a street musician. Put your feet up on your desk and do nothing for ten minutes — or until the rage for motion becomes so overwhelming, your chair can't hold you.

Just before you drift into sleep at night, review your day and some of the decisions you've made. You don't have to judge them. Just recall them. Think about tomorrow. What do you want to do with that day? What prevents you from doing as you will? What one thing could you do to begin to be more truly and happily yourself? Tell yourself that you will do it.

Don't waste yourself "hoping" you'll be a good person tomorrow or that you'll somehow find the power and confidence to be yourself. Declare peace on yourself and on every creature on earth, and go to sleep *knowing* that you will awaken powerful, peaceful and loving.

If you aren't sure how to manage any of this, ask your Big Mind, which surrounds and informs the Little Mind of the masked self, to play with the notion and offer suggestions. When you wake up to those first few minutes of contemplation, without motion or urgency, you'll have an answer. It will be *your* answer.

CHAPTER FOUR

What, me worry?

"Consider the lilies of the field, how they grow.
They toil not, neither do they spin.
And yet I say unto you
that even Solomon in all his glory
was not arrayed like one of these."
THE GOSPEL ACCORDING TO ST. MATTHEW 6: 28-29

How worry steals your time and energy

Worry is a waste of time and energy, a real life-snatcher. It hides in the shadows, disrupts your rest, damages your ability to make decisions, and steals the pleasure and satisfaction you should derive from work and play.

When you worry, you don't plan, work toward a goal, or engage in positive thinking. You obsess on a problem, imagine the worst, fail to make decisions, avoid action.

Worry ignores the present to fuss over a future that never comes. Worry rejects the sweet gift of today to chase the ever-receding horizon of tomorrow. Worry is a substitute for do, an evasion of yes.

Worrying is like paying interest on a debt. You have nothing to show for it, you still have to pay back the principal, and you have no money left for the things you need. Substitute energy and enthusiasm for money and you understand what worry does to you.

Slow down, stop worrying, and you reclaim your life.

"I've always been a worrier," you say. "It's just the way I am." I understand. I've always been a worrier, too. But I've come to realize that we weren't born that way. We learn to worry, learn to expect the worst, learn that we are incompetent to deal with life. And we can learn to replace worry with action and the expectation of positive results.

The world, in the form of parents, teachers and other well-meaning authority figures, sends us lots of worry messages:

- Play it safe. Be careful. Don't take a chance.
- Why even try? You might make a mistake.
- Are you *sure*?
- Don't touch that. You might break it.
- Look both ways — and then stay at the curb.

So we cling to comfort, or even to the discomfort we're used to, rather than risk the failure we've learned to expect. We seek safety and certainty, but we never feel safe or certain. There is no real safety, no final certainty, and to play it safe is to fail to play at all.

If you live for tomorrow — a phantom that exists only in your mind — you fail to live for today, which is rich and real, all you have and all you'll ever need. You need no future to make you whole or to give your life meaning. You are whole in this moment, and your presence needs no explanation, no justification. You have everything you need here and now; you can teach yourself everything you need to know. This isn't wishful thinking. This is the fundamental truth of your existence. You have only to claim it.

That doesn't mean you'll never feel doubt or fear as you face life's conflicts, crises and chaos. You need challenges, and the fear that comes with them. Only when you act in the face of your fear can you grow in wisdom and self-assurance. Without conflict, life would lose its luster.

Instead of trying to evade your fear, acknowledge it as a sign that you are fully alive, and use its energy to empower you to act. You can choose to transform worry into anticipation, fear into excitement. You can convert worry and all its relatives — fear, dread, anxiety and the formless furies — into usable energy.

What are you worried about?

Worry becomes an automatic response. You worry without even knowing it. So again you must seek the wisdom found in slowing down and challenging that automatic response. Give yourself a chance to confront and overcome your fear, so you can try and fail and learn from failure and try again.

In my experience — and I'll pit my anxiety level against anybody's — worries tend to fall into one of three categories:

1. A decision you must make
- big decisions ("Should I be a writer or operate a Service Master franchise?")

- and little decisions ("Should I order a salad with low-cal dress-
  ing or have the double cheeseburger and fries?")

2. An action you must perform
- piano recital
- business presentation
- social gathering

3. An event largely outside your control
- nuclear weapons in Iraq
- holes in the ozone layer
- the endless recession

The worries in the third category tend to be considerably larger (the survival of the planet as opposed to your cholesterol count), but they are also less immediate and therefore probably take up less of your psychic energy than the more proximate concerns. If you worry more about tomorrow's business meeting than about the extinction of the buffalo wolf, that doesn't mean you're a bad person. It just means you're human.

Whatever you're worried about, next time the anxiety erupts, consider these six steps as a way to turn that anxiety into positive energy.

Step One: Don't resist or deny the fear

You'll only send it underground, where it will fester and resurface, stronger than ever, to attack when you're most vulnerable.

Face your fear. Let it wash over you. Feel all of it. As you stop fearing the fear, the panic will subside. Worry will have done its worst.

Step Two: Give the fear specific form and substance

Sometimes fear comes disguised as formless furies, vague dread or anxiety that can shake you out of a sound sleep and leave you wide awake until daybreak. Or it may take on a specific but false aspect. You think you're worrying about the congressional election or the shape your local public schools are in—laudable concerns, to be sure—when you're really worried about the mole on your back that suddenly changed shape and turned red.

You can walk precincts for your favorite candidate and join the local Parent-Teacher Organization, both fine things to do, but you won't stop worrying until you do something about that mole. Track your fear to its

true source. Give it a name. If it helps, write the worry down, as specifi-
cally as you can, on a three-by-five-inch "worry card."

Now you can begin to deal with your fear effectively.

Step Three (optional): Push the fear to the ultimate

The fear doesn't exist apart from you. It's a reaction that takes place
inside you. Since you created it, you can use it, rechannel it or dif-
fuse it.

Let your fear wear your face. Picture it sitting across the table from
you. Ask it the first big question:

What's the worst you can do to me?

If Iraq has the bomb, it could drop it directly on you. If you stumble
and bumble your way through the piano recital, people could laugh and
make rude remarks. If you eat the double cheeseburger and fries, you
could drop dead of a heart attack before getting out of the restaurant.

Now ask the second big question:

What are the odds?

Does Iraq have the bomb (and if so, would it drop it on you)? *Would*
people be that cruel if you butchered your piano piece? (Would you die
of shame if they were?) Okay, you probably wouldn't drop dead right
there in the burger joint, but you might get a bad surprise the next time
you step on a scale.

Step Four (definitely *not* optional): Figure out what, if anything, you can do

Any possible decision you can make must fall into one of these three
categories:

- Do something now.
- Do something later.
- Do nothing.

Deciding to do nothing is different from doing nothing because you
failed to decide. If you examine the situation and determine there's
nothing you can do, you can relieve a great deal of your anxiety. If you
refuse to decide, you'll go on worrying.

Brainstorm all possible options (including options that involve doing
nothing). Play with the possibilities. You could decide, for example, to
seek more information on Iraq's nuclear capabilities and its underlying
philosophy and religion, so you might understand the problem. You
could decide to write a check to one of the organizations that monitors

world traffic in fissionable materials and thus help fight the spread of nuclear weaponry. You could schedule 6:14 A.M. to 6:17 A.M. for concentrated worry about nuclear proliferation and then forget it for the rest of the day.

For that big piano recital, you could leap out of bed immediately and practice until your fingers turn into bloody stumps. You could get up at 4:00 A.M. to practice. You could decide to bag the piano recital and take up the ukelele.

With the burger-versus-salad debate, you could decide to eat the cheeseburger and fast for the rest of the month. You could decide on a compromise — single cheeseburger, with tomatoes and onions, no fries. You could decide to eat the salad but steal bites of your friend's burger.

Choose the option that seems best. Write your decision on the back of your worry card. Then put the matter out of your mind. Every time the worry comes back, gently remind yourself, "I've already decided about that."

You may be wasting a lot of time worrying about decisions you can't make yet. If you toss and turn in bed worrying about *tomorrow's* cheeseburger/salad confrontation, tell yourself "I don't have to decide that now." Say it as often as you need to. Write down the time and place where you will decide. Let your subconscious have the matter for further review.

Tell yourself, "Whatever I decide will be fine." You may have to tell yourself this many times. Tell yourself often enough and you'll begin to believe it, not because you've brainwashed yourself but because your intuition will recognize and respond to the essential truth of the statement.

Step Five: Live with your decision

Make each decision only once. If you decide to eat the cheeseburger, enjoy the cheeseburger. If you decide on the salad, plunge into the salad. If you decide not to eat at all, savor the pleasure of virtuous fasting. Whatever you do, do it wholeheartedly, and then get on with your life.

Step Six: Act in spite of the fear

Since you feel your inner fears but see only the composed masks of others, you may assume that nobody else worries, that you're the only one plagued by formless furies. 'Tain't so. Most folks get them. They can't see yours, either, so they probably figure you're cool and calm unless you choose to tell them otherwise. I learned that for certain when a member of an audience I had just addressed came forward to tell me how dynamic and confident I had been—yet I had gone through several levels of performance-anxiety hell to prepare that speech.

Courage isn't lack of fear. Courage is acting despite and through your fear, rechanneling that fear into energy and alertness. Don't pretend to yourself that you're not afraid. Experience your fear fully. As it runs its course, a gentle calmness will slowly replace it.

Often you must act before you feel confident to act. Take several deep, cleansing breaths. Instead of letting the disaster tapes play in your mind—"moron spills coffee, is struck mute at big presentation in front of CEO"—visualize the event going exactly as you want it to. Expect to be successful. Then act as if you're not afraid.

Sometimes it might even help to admit to others that you're afraid. I remember a particularly anxious moment for my college fraternity brother, Joe Lloyd McAdams. Joe Lloyd was the ace of our three-man free-throw shooting team, and he was good enough to carry us to the university finals. The other team shot first and set a blistering pace. Steve Crowe and I got hot enough to keep us in the contest, but when Joe Lloyd's turn came, he needed twenty-four out of twenty-five to tie and a perfect score to win.

Joe Lloyd took the ball, spun it with his long, slender fingers, bounced the ball once, again, a third time, eyed the basket, and suddenly put the ball on the floor, walked in a tight circle behind the foul line and moaned, "Oh, me. I'm so nervous!"

I figured we were done for.

Joe Lloyd made all twenty-five shots.

I think his open admission of his nervousness helped him do it. Often, now, when I'm faced with a tense situation, I can hear an inner voice with a Tennessee twang saying, "Oh, me. I'm so nervous!" I smile, thank my friend Joe Lloyd for helping me, and get on with it. I don't always shoot twenty-five for twenty-five, but I give it my best shot, pronounce it good enough, and move on.

Shoot if you must this old gray head—but don't make me give a speech

Imagine yourself on the eve of a speech you must give before several hundred strangers. Does the prospect make your palms sweat and your throat constrict so that you can hardly breathe? You're not alone. Opinion polls reveal that Americans fear having to speak in public more than anything else—including debilitating illness, poverty, even death itself.

Let's use America's Number One Fear to illustrate four more important principles for getting worry to work for you.

Let work replace worry

Instead of trying to make yourself sleep when you're terrified, instead of hiding your fear from yourself and those around you, admit your fear and then do everything you can to prepare for the challenge.

If it's a speech that has your pulse racing, prepare the speech meticulously and practice in front of a sympathetic friend, your dog or cat, the bathroom mirror. Practice over breakfast, on the way to work and between appointments. When you feel that the speech is as good as it can get, go through it twice more. This thorough preparation will displace much of your anxiety.

Visualize

As the time of the speech approaches, this exciting double feature probably starts playing in the theater of your mind: "Speaker makes fool of self. Audience performs first public lynching in city's history." If so, book a new movie: "Speaker has rapt audience hanging on every word." Picture yourself giving your speech beautifully. See your audience listening intently.

Get out of the way

Not all of you is afraid—just the ego part, which worries about what others think of you. Gently tell your frightened ego-child, "This isn't about you." Concentrate on what you want to say. Think about the audience members' needs and wants. What will they get for spending their time listening to you? How will your speech make their lives better?

When the ego cries for attention, gently tell it again, "This isn't about you." The more you think about the audience—and the less you think about yourself—the more you'll turn worry into constructive energy.

Imagine a sympathetic audience

Do you go to a speech hoping the speaker will fail? Of course not. You want the speaker to succeed, which is to say, you want her to say something interesting and relevant, in a clear, concise manner. You want to be entertained, informed and enriched.

Most of the folks in your audience feel the same way. They're pulling for you. At worst, they may bring a "show me" attitude, but they'll give you the benefit of the doubt, or they wouldn't have shown up in the first place.

Don't imagine yourself trying to disarm a horde of snarling barbarians with nothing but your voice. Assume you're talking to people who want to hear what you have to say.

Five ways to stop worrying right now

Worry comes in many forms and stems from many causes. Here's a guide to five of the more common subspecies and how to treat them.

1. Worry festering out of ignorance

You can't imagine any good outcome of your present situation. You're either sitting on the horns of a dilemma (two options, both bad) or you're trapped in a box (no options—no way out).

Don't worry. Learn. Seek information. Develop a list of options. There may be several ways off the horns or out of the box. You just don't know enough to see them yet, and your worry prevents you from even looking. As you gather possibilities, don't allow yourself to reject any of them (the automatic "this will never work" reflex). When you've assembled your list, choose the best option and act.

2. Worry lurking in the future

You're worried about a problem but can't do anything about it until later, leaving you with no way to dispel the anxiety now.

Don't worry. Defer.

When you've done everything you can to prepare for tomorrow's challenge, repeat this variation on your mantra: "I can't take that action yet. When I do, things will turn out fine."

Write down the specific time when you'll take action. Then set the problem aside. Every time the worry returns, gently remind yourself that you'll handle it at the appointed time.

3. Worry focused on the past

"I should have. . . ." "If only I had. . . ." "Why did I . . . ?" "How could I have . . . ?"

But you did or you didn't. It's done or it isn't done.

Don't worry. Release.

Is there anything you can do to make the situation better now? If so, write down the action, with the specific time and place you'll do it. Then be sure to keep your appointment, or you'll soon learn to disregard anything you write down on a card.

If there's nothing you can do, or if you decide to do nothing, let it go. I sometimes form a mental picture of my "if only" or "should have" encased in a hot air balloon. I imagine myself letting the balloon go and watching as it rises, becoming smaller and smaller until it vanishes. What image could you use? If imagery helps, use it.

Don't wallow in regret. As fear looks to the future, remorse dwells in the past. They are the same crippling response facing in opposite directions.

4. Worry feeding on inertia

You needed to take immediate action, but you pulled a Scarlett O'Hara: "Tomorrow is another day," you said. But action deferred can be worry compounded. The longer you put off the confrontation, the stronger your worry will become and the harder it will be to overcome it.

Don't worry. Act.

Even a "mistake" is often better than doing nothing. Tell yourself "Whatever I decide will be fine," and act on your decision. If you can't act now, write down the date and place you'll act and the action you'll take. Keep that appointment. Deal with it and get on with it.

5. Worry thriving on evasion

Decisions carry price tags. Whatever choice you make, it will cost you something. You don't want to think about the consequences, so you put off the decision, letting your worry thrive in the vacuum you create.

Don't worry. Pay.

Calculate the cost of your decision as best you can — in time, energy, money and relationships. When you decide on a course of action, decide also to pay the price — and then pay it promptly.

If you don't, you'd better add in the true cost of procrastination. If you put off payment, you'll pay big interest in worry, compounded daily.

Protect yourself from contagious worry

The more you learn about controlling and redirecting your worry, the more aware you'll be of others' futile fretting. You may find yourself surrounded by folks who constantly sing the "ain't it awful" blues. They carp and complain, concoct detailed and vivid worst-case scenarios. Even when they don't, their tension is contagious.

Don't buy into their false sense of urgency. The proprietor of Bill's Key Shop, around the corner from my office, knows how to deal with such tension-generators. A sign posted on the wall by the cash register announces, "Your lack of planning does not constitute my emergency."

Don't try to fix the worriers' problems. They're not really looking for solutions anyway. They just want to complain.

Don't try to argue the worriers out of their worrying, either. No logic on earth can keep up with a worrier who has spent a lifetime turning every "Why don't you?" into an "It won't work."

You can't cure the worrier, but you can protect yourself from the contagion. Announce that you don't want to hear all the blather. That may stun the worriers into silence, at least for a bit. If that strategy fails — as it surely will with some — get yourself out of range of negative vibrations.

Get help if the fears get too big

You can't always fight your worries alone. The techniques we've outlined here will help with the worries most of us encounter. But some folks get more than normal worries. Some develop crippling anxiety attacks that leave them virtually paralyzed. Others see the world slowly close in on them until they're too afraid to venture out of their homes even to run a simple errand.

If your worry falls outside the range of what we might call normal anxiety, seek a doctor's help. Start with your general practitioner or internist, who can direct you to the proper specialist as needed. A combination of therapy and medication may put you back on solid ground and enable you to deal with your fears effectively. I don't make this recommendation lightly. I know that admitting you need help isn't easy. Calling the doctor's office for an appointment—and then keeping that appointment—can be the toughest actions you'll ever take. But that first step can lead you out of your pit and into the sunshine.

Don't try to self-medicate your fear with alcohol or sleeping pills. Your problems won't go away, but your ability to deal with them will. And you'll have added another problem to your list—potential drug or alcohol abuse and dependency. Things will only get worse.

Be gentle with Little Mind

If you didn't know it before, you now know how destructive worrying is. You also know that you can choose not to worry. If you make that choice and keep making it, you can reclaim your life, releasing energy and joy you didn't know you had.

You know all this. You've made out your worry cards. You've repeated your mantras:

I don't have to decide now.
Whatever I decide will be fine.
This isn't about you.

And still you worry. You feel like an alcoholic backsliding from sobriety into the bottle. You're disgusted with yourself. You're ready to abandon all hope of conquering your fears.

Don't. We all worry, including the know-it-all author of this book. Stop beating up on yourself. If you find yourself in the grip of the formless furies, gently lead your Little Mind back to positive, empowering thoughts. If Little Mind insists on showing the disaster tape, patiently rethread the projector and cue up the new feature.

Imagine Little Mind as a frightened child, alone and bewildered by shimmering shadows and strange noises. Embrace that poor child, as you would your own frightened son or daughter, who is terrified by a nightmare and calling out to you for comfort. Tell your child, "Don't be afraid. I'll take care of you."

And know that you will. You can face your challenges and turn your fears into constructive energy.

Owning it

Exorcizing your demons

Here are three exercises to help you confront and dispel your worries.

1. List five to ten actions from your past that you truly regret.
Make a separate three-by-five-inch card for each item. Ask of each regret, "Is there anything I can do now to undo the damage?" If there is, write down exactly what you'll do and when you'll do it on the back of the card.

If you've done all you can, let your regrets go (in little hot air balloons or any other way you choose to send them off). Tear up your card. Scatter the pieces.

2. List five to ten things you used to worry about.
Go back as far as you like, or use worries as immediate as this morning. Take a slow stroll through your list, asking yourself these questions about each entry:

- Am I still worried about this?
- How was the problem resolved?
- Did my worry help in any way?
- Which of my specific actions or decisions helped resolve the problem?
- Did it simply resolve itself?
- Did I just have to learn to live with it?

Review your answers. Do you see a pattern? I suspect you'll discover that worry did little to help, but specific action and the healing power of time may have helped a lot.

3. List five to ten things you're worried about right now.

They can be big or small, global or proximate. It's your list. Make a three-by-five-inch card for each, and ask of each item:

- Will worry help in any way?
- Which actions can I take to help resolve the problem? (Write them on the back of the card.)
- Will the problem resolve itself?
- Will I just have to learn to live with it?

Keep the cards that contain specific actions you've decided to take. Put the other cards in the shredder.

If you can honestly tell yourself that worrying—not deciding, not planning, not acting, but worrying—has helped you in the past or can help you now, go right on worrying. If you can't find any use in worrying, let the worry go and start using all that energy to live instead.

CHAPTER FIVE

How to say "No" to the great distracters

"Is this good news or money?"

MURRAY BURNS ANSWERING HIS TELEPHONE IN *A THOUSAND CLOWNS*

Learning to let the telephone ring

You will declare war in this chapter—not on yourself and your own deplorable "lack of self-discipline," as the clock-racers would have it—but on those people and implements of technology that are robbing you of your time and your life.

Slow down, take a deep breath, understand your options, and then choose how you'll spend your time.

We'll begin with the telephone, number one on my list of examples of technology run amok.

The good slave has become a vicious master

You can stop worrying about ozone depletion, nuclear waste or the destruction of the rain forests. The telephone will probably do you in first. We've let it destroy a part of our environment every bit as precious and perhaps even more vulnerable than our air, water and open spaces—our peace and quiet. In the name of telecommunications, we've forfeited our privacy and relinquished the privilege and the joy of silence.

Alexander Graham Bell's wonderful toy is driving us crazy. It disrupts us at home and at work, demanding that we answer *now*, without knowing who's on the other end.

"Hi. How are you this evening? Good. Have you considered just how beautiful your lawn could look with our scientifically formulated liquid fertilizer and weed-abatement treatment? With just four applications a year, you can turn your drab lawn into a beautiful oasis. . . ."

"I'm calling to ask for your help. We here at the Society to Save the Bulgur Wheat Weevil are asking public-spirited citizens such as yourself to consider making a donation at this critical time. . . ."

"Good evening, madam. Oh. Pardon me, sir. We're conducting a market research survey, and I wonder if you have a few minutes to answer some questions about your beer-drinking habits. . . ."

Sometimes the voice on the other end isn't even human. A computer randomly dials your number, and a computer-generated voice-like synthesizer launches into its pitch, oblivious to your screams or threats.

Phone conversation has somehow become more important than real people. Notice what happens the next time you stand in line at the customer assistance counter and the phone rings. The clerk will answer the phone and deal with the person who isn't there, leaving you and the rest of the folks in line to wait.

We keep answering the bell—leaving food, conversation and love-making to get cold—on the off-chance that we really want or need the call, that it will bring not another intrusion but friendship or love or information.

Perhaps we're simply overawed by the technological. A LaCrosse, Wisconsin, disk jockey tested this thesis by solemnly advising his early-morning listeners to put covers over their phones because the phone company planned to "blow out the lines" that day, and they wouldn't want to get dust all over everybody's homes and offices. Operatives reported walking into offices all over town to find plastic baggies and cloth hoods on all the phones.

We invited the phone into our homes and places of business to serve us. We learned to rely on it. Somewhere along the line, the phone took over. Freed of the lifeline that once tethered it to a jack, cellular phones have migrated into our cars and onto our planes. The newest affront, the pocket phone, weighs in at just 8 ounces and goes anywhere. Fistfights break out in restaurants and theaters, as some spoilsports take exception to having their meal or show disrupted by someone else's arrogance. Experts figure we'll own 33 million pocket phones by the turn of the century, so we can look forward to the phone following us into church, the ball park and other former sanctuaries.

What next? Tele-implants at birth? A permanent phone number tattooed on the wrist? Perhaps a cryptophone, so that even death need not prevent us from reaching out to touch someone.

Who screens for the screeners?

The clock-racers advise you to have somebody screen your calls at work, shifting the burden of the bell onto a secretary or receptionist. But somebody still wastes a lot of time and energy, not to mention the little squirts of adrenaline every time the blasted thing rings. Who's going to screen for the screeners?

And even if you're lucky enough to have someone guard your gate, you've merely postponed the disruption and perhaps made it more unmanageable. Instead of simply answering the phone yourself and taking care of business immediately, you collect all those phone message slips and engage in a stimulating round of telephone-tag, the object of the game being to leave the last message at the end of the day. Tag, you're it.

When I taught at a community college in northern California, my dean of instruction was fond of having his secretary call to announce that the Great One would like to talk to me, and would I mind holding? He called me, mind you, but I wound up holding the phone. It took me a half dozen of these calls to figure out the subtext: He was letting me know that his time was a lot more important than mine.

The next time his secretary called and sweetly informed me that The Big Shot wanted to talk to me, I interrupted her.

"Great," I said. "Have him call me."

I hung up. It felt wonderful.

In a few minutes, the phone rang. It was the dean, sounding a bit chastised, I like to think. He never referred to my little declaration. But he never had his secretary put me on preemptive hold again, either.

With the advent of call-waiting, we can all play the arrogance game, stacking up incoming calls like planes circling O'Hare Airport. "Can you hang on for a minute? I've got a call on the other line."

The answering machine should help us gain control over the telephone by giving us greater power over if and when we receive a call. But the technology works both ways, and you wind up listening to a lot of canned music and trying to cram your message in at the sound of the beep.

"Hi. You're now talking to a machine. Feels pretty silly, doesn't it? We're eating, watching television, making wild, passionate whoopee or any of several dozen other things a lot more important to us than talking to you. If you want to leave a message, make it good, because we might be listening in, and people usually sound pretty dorky on these things." BEEEEEEEEEEEP.

Trying to crack the push-button code on some corporate voice mail machines has become a real challenge. "We're sorry. All our lines are busy right now. If you know the extension of the department you'd like to talk to, and you're calling from a push-button phone, please enter the number now. If you'd like information about schedules, push number one. If you need further assistance, please stay on the line. If you'd like to listen to bland instrumental versions of old Beatles songs, please press number two."

Each new technological marvel comes with the promise that it will simplify life. But each invention seems to add another layer of complexity to the daily routine.

Make a declaration of tele-independence

Perhaps we've forgotten that the telephone — with all its attachments — is just a tool, not an act of God or a force of nature. It's time to put the phone in its place.

Repeat after me: "I don't have to answer a ringing phone."

Say it again: "I don't have to answer a ringing phone."

But what if it's important?

What are the odds?

What if it's somebody I want to talk to?

She'll call back.

Train your friends to call during certain hours. Teach family members to ring twice, hang up, and call back if it's an emergency. Then learn to let the phone ring unless it's convenient for you to answer it.

At first, letting the phone ring may seem like kicking a drug habit cold turkey. But if the phone plays the tune and you do the dancing, it's worth the effort. Choose when you'll talk. Unplug. Establish a quiet, phoneless zone in your day. If answering the phone is an unavoidable part of your job, leave enough margin in your schedule so that calls don't spike your blood pressure and make you run to catch up.

The guest that stayed for dinner — How the unblinking eye wormed its way into the living rooms, dens, kitchens and bedrooms of America

A television set doesn't ring. Nothing happens until we turn it on. But we do turn it on. And we leave it on.

The Average American Household — which doesn't exist, but which may serve as a useful composite — has the television on more than seven hours a day.

For the last thirty years, University of Maryland professor John Robinson has been tracking how Americans spend their time. He concludes that we spend an awful lot of our leisure time watching television — and then complaining about not having enough time.

If you were to log your television time for a week, would you get a nasty surprise? Do you know how much and what you watch? "It's 10:00. Do you know where your mind is?"

Unlike radio, which follows us around and keeps us company while we cook dinner, weed the garden, read and talk, the television squats in one place and attempts to command our full attention. Talk during The Show in some crowds, and you'll get shushed into sullen silence.

But for many of us, television serves as a talking night light, a little noise and a warm glow rather than the focal point of attention. Advertisers have discovered that we remember the general mood of a television commercial but not its factual content — including, in many cases, the name of the product they were trying to sell. When researchers expanded the inquiry to the evening news, they again found only vague comprehension of specifics — this at a time when the majority of Americans now say that television is their primary source of news about the world.

Television is not the enemy

Television is not inherently bad, just as a book is not inherently good. In both cases, the quality of the experience depends on the message, not the medium delivering that message. Television is not necessarily a passive experience, as many have charged, if the viewer's mind is actively engaged in the inquiry.

Television is our national storyteller, the flickering campfire around which we hear our stories. It's a teacher of incredible power. On PBS and MTV, on CNN and Nick at Nite, television is the keeper of our common cultural myths and icons, a part — perhaps the largest part — of our shared heritage. Television has become an integral part of our lives and an element of continuity in an age of rapid change and uncertainty.

When I conjure up memories of family togetherness from my childhood, one of my strongest images is of my parents, my brother and I sitting behind our TV trays, eating soup and sandwiches and watching a quiz show, a situation comedy or a baseball game, the Hollywood Stars taking on the Los Angeles Angels from beautiful Wrigley Field. It's a nice memory.

You could probably list many television shows that have enriched your life. My list would include, in no particular order:

"Gunsmoke"	"The Fugitive"
"Upstairs/Downstairs"	"Hill Street Blues"
"Maverick"	"Beany and Cecil"
"Northern Exposure"	"Crusader Rabbit"
"You'll Never Get Rich — The Phil Silvers Show"	"Soupy Sales"

I won't try to justify my choices on philosophical or sociological grounds (Soupy Sales provided marvelous social commentary and an excellent example of humor operating at child and adult levels simultaneously). I'm not trying to convince you these shows are good. I'm simply saying I like them; they have given me pleasure and even taught me about life.

Your list probably would be different from mine. But if you can make a list, regardless of what's on it, you see some value in watching television.

As with the telephone, though, we must ask, "Who's in charge here?" Especially since the development of the VCR, you can control when and how much television you watch. But do you? Do you watch out of habit or by design? Do you select a show or simply "watch television"?

If your television viewing is indiscriminate, you have a huge source of time to reclaim for other uses — including, of course, reading. And as you control an area of your life that had gotten away from you, you'll also gain the sense of empowerment that comes with any step toward self-mastery.

Television junkies — and the women who love them

When I visited my mom the other day, a woman with curly ringlets of blonde hair was holding forth on the television screen. The words printed at the bottom of the screen said, "Getting married next week, but plans to sleep with other men."

"This is just awful," Mom said, pointing toward the screen.

"I've got a solution," I said, picking up the remote control and pointing it at the screen.

"No, no," she said. "You can't just hide your head in the sand. You have to keep informed."

My question to Mom then, and my question for you now, is "Why?"

I regularly read three daily newspapers, fifteen weeklies and two dozen trade and consumer magazines. I skim, scan and read a couple hundred nonfiction books a year. I study the ballot initiatives and listen to the candidates' debates — no matter how frustrating they are. I read the administration's rationale for the Persian Gulf War and also read a variety of dissenting opinions on our military presence in the gulf. So I "keep up" reasonably well. But for the life of me I can't see why I have to try to keep up on Cher's cosmetic surgeries or Liz's husband du jour.

I also choose not to take the time to try to understand the stock market. I don't know a bull from a bear, a leading indicator from a smoke detector. Seems to me that the market goes up when people think it will — and phone in their "buy" orders — and plunges when people lose confidence in it — precisely *because* they lost confidence in it.

I'm no expert on investments, but I can tell you how the Bakersfield Dodgers did last year, and I can cite Bob "Hurricane" Hazel's batting average for 1957, the year he led the Milwaukee Braves to the pennant. That's the sort of thing I keep up on. One person's trivia is another person's passion.

To some extent, the media set the table for our infomeal. By focusing on sexual harassment, the gatekeepers put the issue on the menu for discussion. By failing for decades to report on sexual harassment, they in effect kept the topic off the bill of fare. Only the concerned, the committed and the highly motivated dug up information on sexual harassment before it became a trendy topic.

You can set your own agenda. Why simply accept what's offered, floating along on top of the flash flood of media infotainment and hype? Fight your way to shore. Seek the information you want and need. Reject the rest. Don't bother feeling guilty if you don't know — or care — about Michael Jackson's new video.

Your own private landfill

You may have already won $10 million!
CARROT APPROACH TO DIRECT MAIL MARKETING

Open this envelope or we'll abduct your firstborn child!
STICK APPROACH TO DIRECT MAIL MARKETING

Direct mail solicitation (a.k.a. "junk mail") comprises a major tributary of the media flood. Starting in late October (the beginning of the "Christmas season" for merchandisers), the outpouring of pitch letters, catalogs and "magalogs" becomes torrential and doesn't let up until the new year (when the bills begin to pour in to take up the slack). Let the mail go for a week and you lose control of your kitchen table or other junk mail holding bin.

We've opened the floodgate by buying more and more by mail. Soon a full 20 percent of retail sales in America will take place via the mail. Even "touchy-feelies," people who traditionally won't buy something they can't fondle, are succumbing to unconditional guarantees of satisfaction.

My two favorite all-time pitches were for the "commemorative" .44 Magnum pistol ("Powerful, *firing* big-bore Magnum honors a *powerful* nation and its *firearms freedom!*") and for a mounted trophy fish that wiggles when anyone in the room talks.

When all those fancy envelopes come to your house, you must at least carry them from the mailbox to the trash—after which, all that glossy paper winds up in the landfill. But most of us sort and read at least some of it. (One recent survey indicated that we open just over 50 percent of it.) And we respond just often enough to keep the flood coming. Direct mail marketers need only a 1 percent to 2 percent response on mailings to make most campaigns a success.

You don't have to spend time reading this stuff just because somebody sent it to you. Be selective. Fight back. Write to the Direct Mail Marketing Association, 6 East 43rd Street, New York, NY 10017 to get off the lists. If the barrage continues, bundle it up and send it back in their postage-paid envelopes. Don't let a pile of irrelevant print demand your time, energy and will.

He ain't heavy—he's just long-winded

Not long ago, a former colleague, now retired, dropped in on me at the office. My heart sank at the sight of him. He's a wonderful man, as kind and honest as any I've ever met, the proverbial pillar of church and community. He is also—there's no nice way to put this—mind-numbingly boring, a real time-eater.

I was busy—when am I not?—in the midst of several projects. Clearly my former colleague qualified as one of the "Very Unimportant Persons" the clock-racers talk about. "Don't even let him sit down," they advise. "Stand up and move to the door. Give him two minutes and out."

But something in his manner made me hesitate. He sat, sighed, and uncharacteristically came right to the point. He was going to have cancer surgery. He wanted me to know. I'm important to him. Would I pray for him?

Life exalts. Life humbles. I gave silent thanks that I had held my tongue. Wasting a little time with a boring friend was by far the best thing I did that week.

But some folks truly do deserve the bum's rush. I include in that category:

- Folks who just need an ear, any ear. If talking to a wall would serve them just as well, let them go find a wall.
- Folks who try to shift their load onto your back. Don't take it, even if you know you can handle the problem more efficiently.
- Folks who want to hand over responsibility for their lives. We can often help our fellow travelers, but we can't fix them, and trying won't help you or them.

- Folks who make unsolicited demands on your time, urge you to "get involved" in their cause and try to make you feel guilty if you refuse. These are the same folks who insisted that you attend the high school pep rally.

If you don't want to shake their pom-poms, you don't have to shake their pom-poms. It might be a great cause. But is it *your* cause? You can only "get involved" in a limited number of worthy causes and still have some life left over. To whom do you owe your time and attention? It's your call. Those who demand—and receive—your precious time simply because you haven't mustered enough courage to turn them away are stealing your life and leaving you with less time and energy to devote to those for whom you feel genuine love and concern. And you're letting them do it.

Are the time-suckers taking advantage of you simply because you can't think of a good excuse to turn them away? *You don't need a reason.* "I don't want to" is reason enough; you don't have to offer explanations.

Owning it

Your personal time-wasters

Make a list of people who eat up your time, your own personal roster of "Very Unimportant People." Are you surprised by the number of names? (Perhaps now you're better able to understand where the time goes.) Next to each name, put a plus, a check or a minus, depending on how you feel about spending your time with that person: a plus for positive feedback, a check for no particular reaction, and a minus for a negative response. Do you spend a lot of time with people you don't like, admire or enjoy? You can choose not to.

Make a second list, folks you hardly ever see but would like to. Can you work some trades here, swapping some of the time you now spend with list A people for time with list B people?

What about other time-wasters? The telephone is my personal number one distracter. What's yours? (Don't include wasters like waiting for the traffic signal to change or sitting in the dentist's waiting room. We'll deal with those in the chapter on waiting.) Can you apply our telephone strategy to these other annoyances? Can you develop other strategies?

What about those time-wasters that have no socially recognized practical value but which you nevertheless choose to do? My list includes:

Reading fiction
Writing a novel about minor league baseball
Writing personal letters
Walking or riding the bike to work instead of taking the bus or
    driving
Taking the long way
Going to movies
Shooting baskets with Jeremiah
Taking long walks with Ellen and Rosie
Petting Ralph and Norton

Just as "I don't want to" is a valid and sufficient reason not to do something, "I like to" is a valid reason to keep doing something that has no practical worth in the marketplace. I won't give up my long walks or my kitten-petting. To do so would be to eliminate some of the little everyday things that give my life its savor.

But if any items on your list have no practical value *and* have no emotional or psychological value for you, strongly consider getting rid of them.

Simplify. Unclutter. Unplug. Take time to choose who and what you spend your time on. Use *your* standards, *your* feelings, *your* intuitions. Only you can define "waste of time" for you. You don't need to justify your choices to those who have little stake in your life but who nevertheless make demands on your time.

CHAPTER SIX

Learning to welcome the wait

"Interruptions are hallowed times."
WAYNE OATES, *CONFESSIONS OF A WORKAHOLIC*

How to turn lost time into some of your best times

Humans seem to be the only critters on earth that defy the law of conservation of energy. When nothing needs to be done — no predator to flee, no prey to pounce on, no natural disaster to escape, no mate to, well, mate with — most of our fellow inhabitants of the planet do nothing. Some do it for months at a time — we call it hibernation, a surefire way to beat cabin fever and the February doldrums. But even when wide awake, most animals spend a lot of time waiting.

And no creature on earth waits better than a dog.

I've had the joy of sharing my life with several wonderful dogs, starting with a black cocker named Cindy, who came into my life when I was four and lived to see me off to college. Ellen and I opened home and heart to a pound puppy we named Buck, who became my kindred spirit for eight too-short years. We took in my mom's miniature schnauzer, Hilda, and liked the experience so much we decided to raise a schnauzer from the ground up and got the incumbent house dog, Rosie.

Maybe they've all been such good waiters because they do so much of it. A house dog's life consists primarily of long stretches of waiting, along with plenty of sleeping, a little eating and sniffing, and brief flurries of frenzy.

Mostly your dog waits for you to pay attention to it — to fill the food dish, throw the ball, tug on the rope, strap on the leash and take a walk. When you're gone, that faithful dog sits in the forbidden chair, looks out the window, and waits for you to come home.

And when you finally return, doesn't he just go stark-raving loony, letting you know that you're the most important creature ever to grace the universe? It doesn't matter what kind of a day you've had or what mood you're in. Your dog doesn't care if you lost the big account, flunked the test or spent six and a half hours staring at a computer screen without coming up with one intelligible word. He's just so glad to see you, he could about expire from joy.

How could you not love something that glad to see you? In the brief moment of mad greeting, your pooch makes up for all the spots on the carpet, all the midnight barking at phantoms, all the trips to the vet, earning a place in the warmest regions of your affection.

Fifteen minutes later, the dog is curled up at your feet, waiting again.

We could all benefit from being a little more like the dog.

Optional waiting—Books, books everywhere, but not a page to read

I just spent forty-five minutes standing in line. I had a great time.

The university bookstore was having one of its 20-percent-off sales. The store announces these sales the afternoon before, and word spreads quickly through downtown Madison. Soon the joint is jammed, lines snaking from the cash registers all the way back to the sociology shelf on the back wall.

I had a clear choice here. Resist the sale and avoid the inevitable wait, or succumb to the sale and endure the wait. I had been eyeing William Least Heat Moon's *PrairyErth* for weeks. I knew right where it was, had cased the shelf several times. The promise of knocking four bucks off the hefty hardbound price pushed me over the edge. I got to the store about 12:30 (I and scads of other lunchtime shoppers), went straight to the shelf, snatched up my treasure, and took up my post at the back of one of the lines.

I opened my book and began to read, becoming almost instantly enraptured by Least Heat Moon's clear, honest style and the accumulation of vast amounts of detail, carefully observed and precisely rendered.

As my line serpentined past other displays of books, I picked up Russell Banks' *The Sweet Hereafter*, and it stuck to my hands. By buying the second book, as any bibliophile will tell you, I saved even more money.

From time to time I looked around at my linemates and noticed that, of the perhaps two hundred people sharing the moment with me, only one other person had opened a book. All those books, all those millions of words, and only two of us reading! Water, water everywhere..... .

Instead of reading, many of my companions were glaring. Some were engaged in heavy, meaningful exhalations of impatient breath. A few were complaining, some quite bitterly, about the wait.

"We chose the slowest line," a woman two spaces behind me lamented. I'll bet folks in the other lines were thinking the same thing.

I'm sure a lot of people left that sale feeling frazzled and frustrated. I returned to work refreshed, having been transported for a while to the unsuspected richness of Kansas, in the presence of a superior storyteller.

That wait was optional. I could have gone back to the bookstore another day, paid a few bucks more, and shot right through the checkout. I chose to wait and save. I paid in time and sore legs. But why should I complain? I made the choice and understood the terms going in. For me, the reward outweighed the waiting. And I made the most of the wait by spending my time in the company of a great writer.

Another study in optional waiting — Peanut butter chocolate chip cookies

I do most of my grocery shopping at Woodman's, a gigantic supermarket (I believe that at one time it was the largest in the United States). It's a great market, full of everything I want. They have the best store-bought peanut butter chocolate chip cookies I've ever encountered. The checkers are usually courteous and efficient. The prices are generally well below the other markets. The checkout counter offers a marvelous array of tabloid trash. ("Gay doc performs sex-change operation on sleeping wife.")

I have to drive several miles to get to Woodman's, and the lines are usually long. But I love those peanut butter chocolate chip cookies, I like the friendly checkers and the lower prices, so I accept the wait as part of the price of doing business at Woodman's.

Again, why complain? You make your choice and you pay the price.

Semi-optional waiting — The long Wisconsin winter

When Ellen, Jeremiah and I moved from California to Wisconsin in 1979, locals took one look at us and told us we'd be lucky to survive the first winter. They weren't far wrong. Ellen and I grew up in southern

California. We knew about body surfing and getting a tan, not about ice skating and avoiding frostbite. Wisconsin in January might as well have been the moon.

We had a lot to learn. The first time the wind chill (a perverse index of human suffering designed to trick you into watching the local weather report) hit −85 degrees, we decided to go to a movie, parked three blocks from the theater, and almost died on the short walk. My toes didn't thaw until the movie was almost over, and when they did, they hurt so much, I thought I might lose them.

The first time Jeremiah and I went cross-country skiing in northern Wisconsin, I managed to pass out from hypothermia, and the poor kid had to half-drag, half-carry me back to the lodge.

I thought storm windows were something you put on when a storm was coming, like "battening down the hatches."

I found that winter presented me with three options:

- I could wait for spring to come — taking away the cold and bringing back my beloved warmth, sunshine and baseball.
- I could wait for winter to be over — burrowing into a warren of bitterness like a hibernating mole.
- I could live the winter, discovering whatever possibilities the snow and ice and cold could offer.

I worked through fear to sullen accommodation and finally to reconciliation. I learned to dress safely and get out into the weather. Just this year — I wouldn't have thought it possible — I found myself actually anticipating winter. It has its joys: the sunrise hitting the new snow; the hoar frost caught in bare tree limbs; the exhilaration of jogging in the bitter cold and the ecstasy of reaching the warmth at home.

Still, we can always change our minds about winter. As we get older, Ellen and I may decide that the icy sidewalks have become too treacherous. Our winter waiting is still optional, although the trade-off for moving to a warmer climate would be rather drastic.

Another study in semi-optional waiting — How time stands still in a doctor's waiting room

You show up at the doctor's office a few minutes early for your appointment, just as you've been instructed to do. You check in with the receptionist and join your fellow penitents on the sinners' bench. And then you wait. And you wait. And then you wait some more. Nobody goes in. Nobody comes out. What are they *doing* in there? Perhaps the doctor sneaked out the back door and is enjoying a quick nine holes of golf.

You don't seem to have a lot of options. Complaining won't speed things up a whit. If you get up and leave, you won't get another appointment for a month.

Finally, you've seen the doctor and have been freed from your waiting-room bondage. You speed back to work, trying to salvage something of the day. As you ease your way into the left-turn lane, your chances for making the signal look good. You're bucking a steady stream of oncoming traffic, true, but only one car squats between you and the intersection. You should be able to make it through on the yellow light (or perhaps just a smidgen into the red) with no problem. But something's wrong. The fathead in front of you isn't easing out into the intersection the way he has to if you're to have any hope of getting through on this light. He's just sitting there. What's the matter with this guy? Did he die behind the wheel?

The signal changes to yellow and then to red. The guy ahead of you doesn't budge. You're stuck for at least one more full cycle of the signal. And who knows? You may be stuck behind the immovable object for months.

You didn't choose this wait, but you must pay for it anyway, in lost time as well as in stress and all the attendant wear and tear on your body and your psyche.

Or do you?

It all depends on your attitude. You can wait in agony for the doctor, inwardly fuming the whole time. You can tie yourself into mental knots over the unbudging car in front of you. Or you can relax and be thankful for the respite, making use of the precious gift of time. It's the same wait, but how you react makes all the difference.

Enforced waiting — Is your mind being held hostage?

As I write this, Terry Anderson is on his way home at last.

For six and one half years, Anderson was held hostage in a land far from his own. His primary "crime" in his captors' eyes was simply being an American. He was chained up most of the time. His life was constantly in danger, and he didn't know if he would ever be free. During the worst times, like the Christmas Day when he broke his glasses, he must have felt his life slipping away from him.

He was denied the most fundamental freedom, the one that forms the foundation for this book: the freedom to decide what to do next.

Reporters asked him how he survived. He said he just got up each morning and did whatever was necessary to get through the day. Sometimes you don't think you can do it, he said, but you do. He kept alert by communicating with fellow prisoners, often using elaborate hand gestures or tapping codes. He read the Bible several times. He made intricate mental plans, including the newspaper he would run just the way he thought it should be run.

Anderson didn't choose his wait, but he endured and even transcended it. He came out vigorous, healthy and fully alive, a testimony to resourcefulness, resiliency and faith in the future in spite of an unspeakable present.

My own enforced wait—Home movies from a summer spent in bed

I've never had to endure anything approaching what Terry Anderson survived. But the summer I turned eleven, I experienced my own enforced wait.

It began with what I thought was a sprained thumb on my left hand, which Dad and I figured I'd gotten playing Little League baseball. My folks had me soak my hand in hot water and Epsom salts every night, as per Doctor Hosepian's orders, but the apparent sprain got no better.

Then one morning I woke up in agony, unable to move without excruciating pain knifing through my body. I had rheumatoid arthritis. Every joint in the left side of my body let me know it constantly.

Dr. H. prescribed aspirin, penicillin and bed rest. Mom provided tons of tender loving care, and Dad managed to arrange his work schedule so he could be with me for all those shots. He also built a special desk on wheels for me to use while bedridden.

When fall found me still unable to get out of bed, the school district sent a home teacher named Mrs. Taylor, a no-nonsense mentor who actually prodded me to do better in school than I had before the illness. A wonderful friend named Craig Marvel visited me every day after school and brought me news of the outside world.

But still, I had a lot of time alone. I read. I listened to Mom's soap operas floating in from the radio in the kitchen. Sometimes I just let my mind drift. I had never been patient, but as a patient, I learned to let life unfold slowly, learned to take it as it came. I measured my recovery in tiny steps, figuratively and in the literal, painful steps of my rehabilitation.

How to turn lost time into good times

Waiting can make you angry and impatient. It can make you stressed and even sick. Or waiting can be an opportunity, an interlude, a bit of found time in an otherwise hectic, overscheduled life.

Your attitude makes the difference. You can't change the wait. You can change the waiting. Here's how.

Accept the wait as inevitable

The world won't rearrange itself for your benefit. You must do some waiting. You can resent it, rail against it, be surprised by it each time. Or you can accept it, use it, turn an annoyance into a pleasure. It's your choice.

Surrender to the wait. Banish the "I'd rather's" or the "I should be's" from your mind. A peaceful mind makes for a short wait, no matter how long the wait actually takes.

Figure the wait into your schedule

Try not to schedule yourself so tightly that a long wait at the doctor's, a traffic jam, or a missed connecting flight can destroy your plans. Figure in slack time. You'll decrease the wait's ability to hurt you and thus defuse your anger.

Give the wait a new name

Do you think of your home as a haven or a hovel? It makes a big difference. We choose names because of the way we feel about the objects they represent. But it works the other way, too. The label you apply can have a lot to do with the way you feel.

Stop calling it a *wait*. Call it a *rest* instead.

The next time you're stuck in traffic, put your mind and body into neutral along with your car. Take several deep, cleansing breaths. Suck the air all the way down to the base of your spine. Let the air out slowly. Focus your attention on it. Let your mind roam to Columbine Lake or Newport Beach or some other nice place it would like to go. Let the tension drain from you. Imagine the strong, knowing fingers of a skilled masseuse kneading those sore muscles.

But don't forget to keep your eye on the road, lest you become the *bonehead* for the impatient driver behind you.

Prepare for the wait

Waiting isn't an activity. It's the lack of activity. Instead of waiting for something to happen *to* you, make something happen *for* you.

Here are a few suggestions, by way of example, for transforming the doctor's waiting room from torture chamber into oasis.

- Bring a friend. Waiting in pairs becomes a chance to visit.
- Bring a book and read your way through the wait.
- Read one of those well-thumbed waiting room magazines. Select one you've never read or even considered reading. I've enjoyed everything from *Good Housekeeping* to *Field and*

Stream and have learned a lot that way.
- Bring a notepad or sketchbook. Write brief descriptions or draw pictures of your fellow waiters.
- Brainstorm potential solutions to the day's problems.
- Plan your dinner menus for the week.
- Work a crossword puzzle.
- Knit.
- Pick a subject and write a haiku about it. (Haiku is a Japanese poetry form consisting of three lines of five, seven and five syllables.) Play with the words until you get something that pleases you.
- Practice your golf swing or tennis stroke.
  Whoa! In the doctor's waiting room? Sure. A lot of coaches prescribe visualization as part of their athletes' training regimen. Picture yourself hitting the tee shot perfectly or handling the backhand from the base line with grace and power.
- Pick a person—anyone in the world, living or dead—whom you would like to talk to. Which questions would you ask? Imagine that person sitting across from you in the waiting room. Ask your questions. Then imagine the person answering them.

Your list of things to do in the waiting room is limited only by your willingness to think about it.

Welcome the wait
If you follow the first four steps, adapting them to your own personality, interests and needs, this last step will be automatic. Not only will you accept the wait; you'll come to anticipate it. You won't be waiting anymore. You'll be whittling or composing a sonnet or taking a quick trip to Bermuda on Fantasy Airlines.

You'll find that you're wonderful company for yourself.

These sorts of midday vacations are so healthy and restful, in fact, that in chapter ten we will explore ways to create them each day, even when you don't have to wait.

Owning it

Things to do instead of waiting

Don't wait until the next wait catches you unprepared. Create your own list of things to do, not *while* but *instead of* waiting. Be as specific as you like. Instead of simply listing "reading," for example, you might select a specific book, one you've wanted to read for a long time but just couldn't find the time for, and make it your "waiting book." The more you wait, the faster you'll get that book read. The more you want to read the book, the more you'll welcome the wait.

CHAPTER SEVEN

Do you really have to hate Monday morning?

"I go on working for the same reason that a hen goes on laying eggs."

H.L. MENCKEN

How to find right work, and how to make work right

I first heard the story of the two ditch-diggers from my father. Seems there were these two fellows working side-by-side, each digging a trench. The sun was murderously hot, the ground hard. A third man approached, watched the men for a moment, and asked the first, "What are you doing?"

The worker stared up at the bystander, leaned on his shovel, wiped the sweat from his eyes and snarled, "I'm digging a ditch. What's it look like I'm doing?"

Undaunted, the inquisitive stranger repeated the question to the second worker.

Without pausing in his labors, the second man smiled and said, "I'm helping to build a cathedral."

How about you? Are you digging a ditch, or are you helping to build a cathedral? Are you shuffling papers or helping an important agency function properly? Are you flipping burgers or feeding hungry people? It isn't the work that creates the stress; it's the way you interpret and react to the work.

Is it bad to work hard? How to tell a workaholic from a hard worker

We toss terms like "addicted" and "codependent" around pretty freely these days. I'm not convinced that "workaholism" qualifies as a genuine disease, but many of us certainly work hard and long, and we pay a price for it. A lot of us:

- work weekends and holidays
- have a hard time unwinding and taking a vacation
- break dates and put off leisure activities to get more work done
- have a hard time distinguishing between "work time" and "time off"

Do you find yourself anywhere in this quick sketch? If you do, is that necessarily bad? It depends. Experts distinguish between happy, productive workers and those whose hard work actually impairs their ability to live full, happy and balanced lives. The happy hard-workers love what they do. They feel a sense of power and control over their lives, and they generally enjoy good health. Perhaps because of this, family and friends tend to accept and support their work habits.

But the impaired workaholic tends to be addicted to the work itself — not the results it produces — and works in a compulsive, obsessive manner. The "to-do" list becomes an imperative, not a guideline. Deadlines produce panic and frenzied, often wildly inefficient bursts of activity and emotion. A missed deadline is a disaster for the workaholic and for anybody near enough to catch the fallout.

To know whether your work habits hurt you, ask yourself these questions:

- Do you ignore unmet needs and sacrifice relationships because of your work?
- Do your family and friends suffer because of your work habits?
- Do you resent the time spent working?
- Does work leave you exhausted?
- Could all that busyness at work be in some sense an escape from other responsibilities?

If so, it doesn't really matter what you call it. You've got a problem, and you need to seek a better balance in your life between work and rest, creating enough time for relationships and other interests.

Finding right work — Making pictures and writing stories

Vern Arendt grew up on a family farm near Cedar Grove, Wisconsin. At age twelve he blew his life savings, $5.10, on a folding camera that fit neatly into his overall pocket. He had to wait two months to save up thirty cents more to buy a roll of film and another month after that to save the quarter it cost to have his first twelve photos developed.

"There wasn't a bad picture in the bunch," he says.

He was hooked.

He landed a job as staff photographer for a weekly newspaper and has been there for thirty years. For Arendt, photography is vocation, avocation and hobby all in one. He does what he loves.

Was Arendt born with a special talent for photography? Could be, although scientists haven't isolated the shutterbug gene on the DNA chain yet. Whatever the origin of his urge to pick up a camera and make pictures, Arendt was wise enough to follow his instincts and devote his life to doing what he loved and was naturally good at.

National Book Award-winning author Herbert Kubly, another Wisconsin farm boy, needed a bit of help to pursue his right work. From an early age, Kubly knew he wanted to be a writer. He sneaked off every chance he got, to read and to write his stories. Local folks told Kubly's father he had a lazy son, one "too dumb" to be a farmer. But Kubly's father understood and, by letting his son skip chores to pursue his dream, "he was giving me permission to write," Kubly says.

But what if folks like Kubly and Arendt don't receive permission or aren't brave enough and wise enough to follow their hearts to the work they're meant to do? The result can be tragic, as Arthur Miller dramatizes in his play, *The Death of a Salesman*. The protagonist, Willie Loman, was "a happy man with a batch of cement," and there was "more of him" in a back porch he had added onto his house than in all the sales he ever made. But because he had learned that "menial labor" was beneath him, he didn't allow himself to pursue the work he loved. Instead, he spent his life pursuing "success" in something he couldn't love and wound up deciding he was literally worth more dead than alive.

"Without work, all life goes rotten," Albert Camus wrote. "But when work is soulless, life stifles and dies."

Making work right — Romancing the news

Veteran editor Clarke Stallworth likes to tell young reporters, "You are God's chosen people."

Some laugh, but Stallworth isn't kidding.

"Reporting is a license to have some fun," he says. "You get paid to run around asking questions and learning things."

Nobody knows better than Stallworth how tough writing on deadline can be. He served as city editor at the Birmingham, Alabama, *News* for thirteen years and then as managing editor for four more. Yet he calls the news business "a romance."

Stallworth has obviously found his right work. But he also had to make the work right, transforming his function at the *News* from editor to coach.

"I used to be a champion newspaper tearer-upper," he says. "Somebody would hand me some copy, and I'd tear it up big time. And they'd hate me for it."

He had a conversion experience, he says, learning to work *with* instead of *against* his reporters. He learned to ask questions and do a lot of listening, so that the reporters could make their own stories better.

"A good editor can fix copy," he says. "A great editor can help people grow."

A worker with a shovel can dig a ditch. A worker with a vision can help build a cathedral.

Inventing right work—Montana Monster Cookies

John Thiede's ideal job didn't exist until he invented it for himself.

Thiede came from Florida to the plains of Montana to become a landscape architect and to work under those big skies Montana is famous for. He wound up baking cookies.

Work was scarce for a would-be landscaper. He thought of returning to Florida, where the burgeoning population would provide more career opportunities. But Thiede had fallen in love with Montana and wanted to stay. He was big and strong—had in fact played college football—so he worked construction to put food on the table. To supplement his income, he and his sister started baking cookies, using an old family recipe.

This wasn't just any cookie. This was a huge, warm embrace of a cookie, a blend of chocolate chips, raisins, peanut butter and oatmeal that dares you to try to eat more than one at a sitting, a cookie worthy of the name Montana Monster.

Thiede baked at night, renting ovens at a bakery in Livingston, and then drove down the Paradise Valley into Yellowstone Park, dropping off packages of his cookies at the little stores that agreed to carry them.

Word spread. Cookie lovers began asking for Monsters, and soon Thiede was having trouble keeping up with demand. Something had to go, the Monsters or other career ambitions.

Thiede plunged into cookie dough full time. He bought out his sister's share of the operation, renovated a store on Main Street, and began baking cookies as if his life depended on it—which it did. He found that he liked running his own business and liked serving the people who came to the store. He installed a bench outside the shop, so folks could sit and watch the world go by while enjoying their cookies. Sometimes Thiede, busy as he was, would come out and sit with them.

He invented new facets of his business. He began carrying other Montana products and found that he could sell his goods through the mail. Instead of a regular catalog, he developed a newsletter, full of stories about local doings in and around Livingston (including the sighting of a bear on Main Street). The business thrived on Thiede's inventiveness and hard work, and soon he had to move to larger quarters on Interstate 90.

Thiede loves his work. And why not? He invented it. Nobody asked him to start baking his cookies, and nobody assured him of success when he did. Thiede created a place for himself, so that he could live where and how he chose.

Merging work, values and family life

Dave Ramey recently walked away from a job as president of a large conference center in Dayton, Ohio, to devote full time to his growing consulting business, Strategic Leadership Associates.

He made the leap without a net. Ramey's wife, Mary, a counselor and therapist, had just gone back to school to earn her doctorate. The oldest of the Ramey's four kids was about to start college. Ramey's job offered steady, secure income to finance the family's various pursuits. But Ramey needed more than steady and secure. He needed his work life to mesh with the values he has spent his adult life building. In his words, he wanted "a clearer fit . . . to achieve larger goals."

Paying attention to his values and making work correlate with those values "doesn't eliminate suffering," he admits. "It doesn't eliminate adversity. It doesn't make things go easier. It just is the right way to do it."

Ramey says he pays attention to the two fundamental principles of balance and diversity, devoting time and energy to family and personal development as well as work.

In a journal Ramey has kept almost daily for years, he reviews his activities in light of his goals and eliminates those that don't contribute. That allows him the time not only for creative thinking but for "taking a walk in the woods . . . or talking to my children about basic values," he says.

"For me, working at that larger process of lifework . . . is the top priority," Ramey concludes. "I do not count hours, minutes, projects, tasks or even accomplishments. . . . The less I concentrate on these things, the more it seems that satisfaction has come in my direction."

Some, like Vern Arendt and Herbert Kubly, find their right work early on. No identity crises for these folks. Others, like Clarke Stallworth and Dave Ramey, must make the work right. And still others, like John Thiede, must create the work from scratch. In each case, they had to back up the decision with hard work and the courage to follow the vision.

Being ground down by work

These work experiences are a long way from those of my grandfather, Arthur Cook. A silkweaver by trade, he immigrated from Belgium and settled in Paterson, New Jersey, where he went to work in one of the huge weaving mills along the mighty Passaic River. The work was grindingly difficult, working conditions miserable, pay meager.

Nobody asked Cook or his fellow weavers if they were satisfied with their "career choice." He worked so he and his family (which on Christmas Day, 1906 grew to include my father, George) could survive. He even had to take his daughter, Susan, out of school when she was just thirteen and bring her into the mills with him.

The mill workers eventually rose up in one of the most famous strikes in American labor history, demanding an eight-hour day and a minimum salary of twelve dollars per week. They achieved neither, and the bitter five-month strike was a factor in the rapid decline of the silkweaving industry in America. Today all those factories along the Passaic River are abandoned. But brutal working conditions remain— for miners, for assembly-line workers, for migrant farm workers and for many others.

Does your work make you sick?

Most folks don't have to work as long or as hard as did the silkweavers of Paterson, New Jersey, at the turn of the century. In fact, compared to the working conditions many of our ancestors endured, most of us have it easy. But even so, many of us don't feel the way Clarke Stallworth, John Thiede, Herbert Kubly or Vern Arendt do about their work.

"I'm convinced that the majority of decent, average, conscientious men of business put not as much but as little of themselves as they conscientiously can into the earning of a livelihood," wrote Arnold Bennett back in 1910, "and that their vocation bores rather than interests them."

Researchers at the University of Michigan surveyed 1,533 American workers on their attitudes toward work. When asked if they'd choose the same type of work again, 93 percent of university professors said they would. Journalists were almost as enthusiastic, 82 percent reaffirming their career choices. Few Willie Lomans in these groups. (The odds of liking my work were in my favor when I chose a career as teacher and journalist.)

But only 43 percent of folks in the general category "white collar worker" said they'd do it over again, and the percentages fell to 24 percent for blue collar workers, 21 percent for unskilled steelworkers and 16 percent for unskilled autoworkers.

Researchers also asked workers what they considered to be the most important elements of a good job. You might guess that they'd respond "good pay," "short hours," "easy work" and "job security." If you did, the results will surprise you. The most important elements, the workers said, were: (1) interesting work and (2) the equipment, information and authority necessary to do the job right. The opportunity to develop skills and abilities also placed high on the list. Good pay finished a weak fifth, job security seventh.

These folks don't want it easy. They want challenge, and they want the tools and the freedom they need to meet the challenge.

And if they don't get these things, their work could even make them sick, according to Dr. Kenneth Pelletier, an expert on stress in the work place. Just as school motivates many children to feign and even develop illnesses, the work place "provides strong incentives to sickness," Pelletier says. It's no coincidence that the most perilous time for heart attacks and strokes is 9:00 A.M. Monday.

Getting to do "whatever you want"

If you have a great deal of freedom in structuring your workday, can take responsibility for the outcome, and can see the value in what you do, you're more likely to achieve satisfaction from your work. If you have little freedom, are simply a fragmented part of a much larger and largely unknown process, if your labors seem to matter little in the final product, then the work will not be sustaining.

I became aware of how important my freedom on the job is to me one day several years ago, when I took my son Jeremiah to work with me. He was then about ten years old, and he busied himself with stapler, hole punch, copy machine and other office toys.

About midway through the afternoon, he looked up from his play and asked me, "Do you get to do whatever you want to?"

My first impulse was to say, "Of course not! This is work!" But I realized that nobody had come in all day to tell me what to do or how to do it, and Jeremiah had noticed.

"Yeah," I finally replied. "In a way, I guess I do."

I felt a warm rush. How good that is—the simple freedom to plan out your day's work and to take responsibility for the results. I realized that "work" didn't really seem separate from the rest of life for me but was more a natural part of the flow of the day.

That feeling gives me a distant kinship with the early hunters and gatherers, who had no separate word for "work." Getting and preparing food, making tools and clothes, building a shelter were simply a part of what you did and who you were. Questions such as "Does your work fulfill you?" would have made no more sense to these people than the question "Are you satisfied with the way your stomach digests food?"

But as we evolved from hunters and gatherers into CPAs and construction laborers, we became physically, emotionally and psychologically alienated from our work. We began to define "good work" as "less work." We began to horde leisure time as "our" time and to resent the time we owed to somebody else in exchange for a wage.

More and more of us are pouring more and more of our time and energy into jobs, not out of a love for the work, but out of economic necessity or because we've become trapped in what researcher Juliet Schor calls "the earn and spend cycle."

How to find your right work

Somewhere between the work shirker, who resents the job and puts as little into it as possible, and the impaired workaholic, who works with frenzied compulsiveness, you can find that happy convergence of right work and positive attitude. Preference tests and guidance counselors may help you in your search, but no one can tell you what's right for you, and you should accept no one's opinion as truth. The answer is inside you. You need to discover it for yourself, and you must be willing to spend whatever time and energy the search demands.

One of my students recently demonstrated the kind of will such a search requires when she wrote, "I don't want to fall into my life. I want to make it happen."

Discernment and fulfillment come in four stages. They are easy to list. They aren't easy to do.

1. Know who you are.
2. Choose what is right and true for you to do with your life.
3. Believe that you will be able to do it.
4. Be willing to pay the price for your choices.

Find work that matches your disposition, your aptitudes, your interests and your values. Follow your inclinations and intuitions. Heed the urgings of your heart. Seek the right way—not the safe way, the easy way or the accepted way.

If you love what you do, you'll be good at it. If you're good at it, you'll be a success at it. You may not necessarily make a huge amount of money (some "right work" pays better than others), but we're talking about making a life, not making a fortune. You'll find a way to make a living, and that living will feed you with energy and satisfaction as well as bread, and it will not be separate from the rest of your life.

Reaffirming right work—How momentum almost carried me into court

Like Vern Arendt and Herbert Kubly, I knew what I wanted to do in life from a very early age. But I almost lost my way.

I've always wanted to be a writer. Oh, sure, at various times I've wanted to be the Lone Ranger, Hopalong Cassidy or Superman, and I wanted to pitch for the Dodgers. Still do, truth to tell.

But I liked to smell newspapers even before I could read them. My grandfather, William Gilmore Beymer, was a writer and a journalist, and I'd sit on the floor in his den and watch him at his desk, amid the clutter of books and yellow second sheets and pipe tobacco. Writing words and then seeing them in print seemed to me then and seems to me now to be just the best job possible. I've never analyzed that notion, but I felt it strongly.

I majored in creative writing in college because all I had to do was write short stories and occasionally have them torn to shreds by my classmates. I also got credit for reading novels and short stories, which I wanted to do anyway.

I took a class from Wallace Stegner, as much of a craftsman talking about the short story as he is writing them, and something stirred in me that said teaching writing wouldn't be so bad, either.

Having no desire to leave the university and start earning a living at such a tender age, I went on for a master's in journalism. Again they gave me credit for doing things I liked to do anyway. My advisor and mentor, Bill Rivers, was a passionate and brilliant writing teacher, and he taught me as much about teaching as he did about writing.

I still shied away from that cliff-marked "real world," so, for want of something better to do, I took the law boards, did well, and enrolled at Hastings College of the Law in San Francisco. My soon-to-be bride, Ellen, helped me land a job at the University of Santa Clara, teaching one class of composition, which barely covered food and the rent on an unfurnished apartment near the university. I furnished it with a sleeping bag, two TV trays and a tiny, black-and-white television, on which I watched "Hondo" (a largely unappreciated classic starring Ralph Taeger) every Friday night. I taught my class at 8:00 A.M., caught the commuter train for the city, sat in my law classes, studied on the train home, prepared classes and read more law at night. I liked my life, and I liked learning law by the case study method, as much an education in history and human nature as in law.

But one day I broke stride and stopped to take a breath. I lost the momentum that had carried me from first grade all the way to law school and would have carried me straight into a legal career. I felt as if I'd been shaken awake right in the middle of Professor Prosser's torts class. As I looked around at my fellow students, a question formed in my mind, as clearly as if someone were speaking the words in my ear:

"Do you want to be a lawyer?"

Hadn't occurred to me to ask myself that.

You will get no lawyer jokes here. There are sleazy lawyers, yes, but there are also dedicated and creative ones. If we have become a litigious society, we must blame ourselves, not the folks we hire to sue one another. But the question before the house wasn't "Do you like lawyers?" or "Do you admire lawyers?" or even "Do you think being a lawyer is an okay job for somebody to have?" all of which I probably would have answered in the affirmative. The question was:

"Do you want to be a lawyer?"

My answer was *"No."*

What did I want to be? I wanted to be a writer. And as bad as I was at it at first, my 8:00 A.M. class at Santa Clara was confirming in me a love for teaching writing as a wonderful way to support the writing habit. My old passions stirred. I wanted to be a writer and a writing teacher.

God gave me a sign. A member of the English faculty died, and I was given his classes. I taught full time at Santa Clara for three years, went on to Solano College and taught for eight more, gaining tenure and becoming department chair. I had a wonderful time in the classroom and developed strong friendships with several wonderful colleagues. I could have stayed there for life.

Finding right work for two—Holding hands as you jump off the cliff

Meanwhile, my wife Ellen had followed her own inner urgings into a job as director of religious education for a parish in Napa, where we lived. We both liked our jobs a lot. We are native Californians, and we enjoyed the good life in the wine country. We felt secure—maybe too secure. We began to worry that we had learned all we could where we were.

And my administrative duties were pulling me more and more away from the classroom and leaving me with less and less energy for writing.

We cast about for other opportunities, and Ellen received first an interview and then an offer of a great job as director of special religious education for the diocese in a place called Madison, Wisconsin, located on some sort of alien planet covered with snow and ice.

We left family, security and our known world and moved to Madison, where I had no job at all but figured to find out if I could make it as a freelance writer. Ellen plunged into her new challenge, and I began collecting rejection slips, getting an occasional piece in print and spending a lot of time with son Jeremiah, exploring our new world.

As I walked through the door and into Lowell Hall to interview for a job as a half-time program coordinator for the University of Wisconsin-Extension's journalism department, I felt a sense of peace, certainty and strength. I knew I would get the job, and I knew the job would work out well for me. I had no reasons to support this feeling. I just knew. I got the job, worked it into full time, began doing some teaching, and eventually got on the tenure track.

I'm now a full professor and enjoy a lively freelance career, which feeds my teaching and enhances my credibility as a writing coach. Lately I've even gotten to write books about writing. I teach journalism on campus and get to work with newspaper folk all the time. I love my work. It's much more than a job to me. I pour a lot of myself into my work, and in a sense I think I even lose myself in my work sometimes. But I find a happy and productive new self. I think I'm good at what I do, and I think that's because my work reinforces my inclinations, draws on my aptitudes, and meshes with my goals and values.

How to make work right

I created the job I now enjoy so much, but I know how lucky I am to have it. Many jobs are repetitious, unchallenging, seemingly meaningless, even life-denying. I've had a few of those jobs along the way myself. I've pushed buggies full of wet concrete in the southern California heat for ten hours without a break, which was physically exhausting. I've stood for thirteen hours a day in the same heat outside a Mayfair market, asking people about their beer-drinking habits, which was soul-numbing.

I learned that my attitude could transform the reality. It makes a tremendous difference whether I'm pushing a concrete buggy or helping to construct the (then) tallest building in Los Angeles.

You see the difference attitude can make every time you shop. Some cashiers make you wait while they finish their conversations with coworkers. They don't know their merchandise. They don't know how to work the register. They pop gum in your face. In dozens of ways they make it quite clear to you that they're simply putting in time, you're interrupting them, and they just don't care about you. They can make you miserable if you let them. And they make themselves miserable, all day, every day.

But others in the same situation will greet you with a smile, work with speed and efficiency, answer and even anticipate your questions and in every way make your encounter with them pleasant and even uplifting.

At a restaurant in Bountiful, Utah (a beautifully named and quite pleasant suburb of Salt Lake City), a waitress brought my wife the wrong breakfast order. When we politely (I hope) pointed out the error, she checked her ticket, shoved it in Ellen's face, and said, "Nope. Here it is, right here. Short stack." Meaning, apparently, that Ellen was to stop complaining and eat the pancakes she hadn't ordered.

We insisted (again politely, I hope, but it was getting tougher) on getting the food we wanted instead of the food the waitress seemed determined to bring us. With much grumbling and muttering, the waitress at last surrendered. She had lost another battle in what must seem to her to be an endless war.

But at another restaurant, this one in Kadoka, South Dakota, a waitress named Phyllis relieved our road-weariness with friendly conversation, brought our orders promptly, made us feel welcome.

We left Bountiful a bit more tense than when we had arrived. We left Kadoka refreshed.

I'll just bet Phyllis enjoys her job and leaves work with enough energy and pep to enjoy the rest of her life, too. It's all in the attitude.

Owning it

A five-step process for making work right and finding right work

Here are two steps that can help you create a positive attitude about your job and three more to help you find or create a more fulfilling job.

See the big picture
Don't check your brains at the door. Seek information that teaches you how your tasks contribute to the larger objective. Discover how your

work ultimately translates into a benefit in someone's life. Seek ways to make your labor even more beneficial.

Become constantly better at what you do

When I got a job as a construction laborer, I was scared that I wouldn't be able to measure up physically. I had attained my full height but weighed about 150 pounds, most of it in my head and feet, so I had reason for concern. But I was disdainful of any potential challenge to my intellect.

I was wrong. Turns out that digging a firm trench with squared edges requires technique. I was humbled. I had to learn a lot just to become competent.

Even if you're already good at your work, constantly seek ways to be better. Learn new facts about your product or service every day. Use every spare moment for exploration and discovery.

These two steps can transform your daily grind into a stimulating adventure. They'll also transform you into a more valuable employee. What's good for you will be good for the boss, who in turn may reward you. But even if you receive no praise or pay raise, you'll transform your attitude about your work and thus transform the work itself.

Look for and create opportunities

The university hired me to rent rooms, count chairs, order meals, compute costs and fill out paper work. My boss called me "Highly overqualified." I agreed. When I finished my assigned tasks, I read books, conducted surveys, sat in on workshops, began making suggestions, and in time worked myself into the job I now have and thoroughly love.

Look for and create ways to do more. You'll work harder, but it won't seem like it, because you'll feed your curiosity and your hunger to do something worthwhile.

And again, what's good for you will be good for the boss (unless you appear to be after the boss' job!).

Make a plan

Perhaps you're carrying out steps one, two and three, and it's making a big, positive difference in your work life. But still, you know that this job isn't what you want to spend the rest of your life doing. If that's the case, figure out what you really want to do. This may take a lot of thought, perhaps some study, maybe even some counseling. Whatever it takes, do it. The time you invest in yourself now can pay tremendous dividends later. You're worth the time and effort.

Based on your conclusions, develop a plan. How can you get from where you are to where you want to be? How long will it take? Will you need new skills or knowledge? How can you get them?

You won't leap there in a single bound. You'll probably accomplish most of the changes one small step at a time. List as many of the intermediate steps as you can anticipate. As you accomplish each step, no matter how insignificant in itself, you'll know it's part of the plan. You'll know where you're heading, and your life will have a purpose.

As you figure out what it will take to get you where you want to go, also compute the price tags, as well as you can anticipate them. What will these steps cost in time, effort and money? What won't you be able to do while you're doing the new and necessary things?

As you change your life's direction, you may also need to change your attitudes. You may have absorbed the notion, for example, that work you do at home isn't "real" and doesn't "count." Unless you challenge such an attitude, it can prevent you from setting up a home office or staying home with the kids while your spouse brings in a paycheck.

If your plan doesn't feel right, figure out whether you'll need to change your plan, your attitude or both. But don't let conventional wisdom prevent you from embracing the work that's right for you. It doesn't matter what "they" think. What do *you* know?

Do something *every day* to work toward fulfillment of your plan
Read a book, talk to a knowledgeable co-worker, begin or continue to learn a new skill—do something each day that moves you closer to where you want and need to go.

But don't live only for that future goal. Enjoy the day and the tasks in it fully, for themselves.

At the end of each day, take a moment to remind yourself of what you've accomplished in terms of your goals. Then think about what you'll do tomorrow and how well you're going to do it.

CHAPTER EIGHT

Weapons in the war on stress

"I like to be pushed. I like to be challenged. I like to go the limit."

JULIO VEGA, COOK, CENTER COFFEE HOUSE, 51st STREET, NEW YORK CITY

How to ease your body and your mind

Feeling stressed out? You're not alone. Counselors and psychologists across the country report a big jump in complaints of stress, burn-out and even severe anxiety disorders. Treating stress has become a growth industry, with folks offering pills and potions, massages and mantras, retreats and renewals.

Most of us seem to accept stress as the normal state of being. Some even wear "executive syndrome" stress symptoms as a kind of badge of courage. If you're not stressed out, you must not be pulling your oar.

Last chapter we met some people who found or created jobs that offer them emotional satisfaction and a sense of worth. But most folks feel stressed, not satisfied, at work, judging by a recent survey by the Northwestern National Life Insurance Company. The survey reported that one of every three Americans considered quitting their jobs in the previous year because of work place stress. Seven out of ten surveyed said job stress caused frequent health problems and made them less productive.

How does your job rate on the stress scale?

Another recent survey, published in *Men's Health* magazine, listed the most stressful jobs as follows: (1) inner-city school teacher; (2) police officer; (3) air traffic controller; (4) medical intern and (5) firefighter. No surprises here. These folks are obviously under a lot of pressure on the job. Securities trader, urban bus driver and roofer also scored high on the stress scale.

But the sixth-, seventh- and eighth-place finishers are a little harder to figure: waiter, assembly-line worker and customer-service representative. Middle-level manager, salesperson and banker also scored high. Why are these folks so stressed out?

It's a matter of control. The folks who treat high blood pressure and other stress-related diseases report that the patients with the biggest health problems see themselves as having little control over their lives. Black blue collar workers tend to get more heart disease than do white CEOs, for example.

Job stress isn't confined to an office. Upper Midwest farmers committed suicide—surely the ultimate stress response—at a rate about double the national average during the 1980s—years plagued by drought, plunging land values and sliding commodity prices, all factors out of the farmers' control.

What's your stress point count?

Factors other than the job contribute to stress, of course. Two scientists named Holmes and Rahe in 1967 developed a rating scale to assign "stress points" to specific life events. Rack up 150 points in a year, they discovered, and you stand a good chance of racking yourself up with a stress-related illness.

The top six items on the Holmes-Rahe Social Readjustment Rating Scale offer no surprises:

Death of a spouse	100 points
Divorce	73
Marital separation	65
Jail term	63
Death of a close family member	63
Personal injury or illness	53

These are all pretty rough experiences, and we'd expect them to be stressful. The only mystery about number eight, "fired from work," is that it doesn't score higher than 47 points. Maybe they were relieved to be out of a job they hated.

But item seven on the list, weighing in at a hefty 50 stress points, is marriage. All jokes aside about marriage being equivalent to getting thrown in the slammer, isn't it supposed to be a positive event?

That's the point. Even good change is stressful. At 45 stress points, marital reconciliation is only 20 points less stressful than marital separation. Retirement tallies 45 stress points, and an addition to the family, usually considered a "blessed event," scores 39 points. Even "outstanding personal achievement" costs 28 stress points.

A spouse beginning work is just as stressful as that same spouse quitting work (26 points). Finishing school is just as stressful as starting (26 points). A change, any change, in work responsibilities is worth 29 points, and any change in living conditions scores 25. Moving to that dream house in the country will cost you 20 stress points. Vacation tallies 13 points, and Christmas is right behind with 12.

Any change is stressful, which means that, unless you fall into a coma, stress is unavoidable. The trick is in learning to deal with the stress.

Bringing the stress scale up to date

Psychologist Georgia Witkin recently readjusted the scale to reflect more accurately the life women lead in America today. Death of a spouse still leads her list at 99 points, with divorce second at 91. Getting married places third with 85 points, being fired rates 83, and pregnancy and marital separation both merit 78 points.

Christmas has climbed way up the stress ladder, soaring to 56 on Witkin's scale. "Sex difficulties" has shown a less-dramatic but nevertheless significant increase, up from 39 to 53. Stress still gets us coming and going. Addition of a new family member scores 51 on Witkin's scale, while a son or daughter leaving home is worth 41.

Stress isn't "out there"—it's "in here"

We usually use the term "stress" to mean "hassles" or "pressure." But according to Hans Selye, one of the founders of stress research, stress isn't an external event; it's inside us, our body's response to the demands put on it. It isn't the deadline, the divorce or the death of a loved one; it's the way our bodies react to these life events.

Selye described the stress response as a cycle of alarm, resistance and exhaustion. He studied this cycle by putting mice in a refrigerator to see how they would adapt to a severe and stressful change in the environment. At first the mice cowered in the corners, but they soon adapted beautifully and seemed to thrive in their new, frosty home. But if Selye left them in the refrigerator too long, they all suddenly died. Selye concluded that short-term stress can be exhilarating, bringing out our best in response to the challenge. But long-term, unrelieved stress can be a killer. Stress seems to be an extreme example, then, of the law of diminishing returns.

Juuuuuuust enough stress

Too much stress can make us sick and maybe even kill us. But too little stress can be almost as bad, leaving us bored and unproductive. Just enough stress, a state Selye calls "eustress," keeps us healthy and productive.

So like Goldilocks and her famous bowls of porridge, we want life to be "not too hot, not too cold, but juuuuuuust right." The amount of stress needed to produce this just-right state of eustress varies from person to person. But for all of us, it's not the situation but our reactions to the situation that count.

Good stress can bring out our best

Professional athletes perform under unusually stressful conditions. When most of us make a mistake at work, only a few people know about it. When a three-million-dollar-a-year slugger strikes out, thousands boo him, and millions more read about it the next day. Strike out enough times, and that slugger no longer commands the big salary.

But the true star seems to thrive on pressure. Former Los Angeles Laker guard Jerry West earned the nickname "Mr. Clutch" for his ability to sink the game-winning shot with a championship on the line, even if that shot happened to be a desperation heave from well beyond the half-court line. The greater the pressure, the more West wanted the ball. He was supremely confident in his ability to respond to the situation.

Boston Celtic basketball star Larry Bird describes the effects of "good stress" this way:

> I remember the first time we won, against Houston [in 1981]. We were way ahead at the end, and so I came out with three minutes left, and my heart was pounding so much on the bench, I thought it would jump out of my chest. You know what you feel? You just want everything to stop and stay like that forever.

But if it did, Selye warns, good stress, which results in peak performance, would turn to bad stress, which leads to sickness and even death.

Bad stress can make you sick

During the stock market plunge of October 1987, 116 stressed-out traders on the floor of the stock exchange came down with mumps. Coincidence? Most likely not. Researchers now say that stress can increase our susceptibility to a wide variety of diseases, including rheumatoid arthritis, high blood pressure, various infections, allergies, and even some forms of cancer.

Dr. Christopher Coe, a professor of psychology at the University of Wisconsin-Madison, may have figured out why. In his research, he separates young rhesus monkeys from their mothers and measures the physiological changes that result. (It's better than popping rats into the deep-freeze, I suppose.) Coe reports a reduction in the number of white blood cells and a decrease in the functioning of the cells that remain in the emotionally distressed monkeys. White blood cells are the body's primary means of fighting off disease. A decrease in healthy white blood cells leaves the body more vulnerable to sickness.

Coe and other researchers are finding clear evidence of interaction between our behavior and the chemical reactions in the brain that govern the way the body functions. This complex relationship goes by the mind-boggling term *psychoneuroendocrinology* – the study of the interrelations of psyche, brain and body chemistry.

Here's an example of the kind of relationship this new branch of science is uncovering. When you're placed under stress, the brain releases several chemicals to prepare the body to respond, the so-called "fight or flight" response. Adrenaline is the best known of these chemicals. The brain also releases cortisones, which scrape the inner walls of the arteries as they surge through the body. The body tries to repair these potentially dangerous arterial lesions with a substance called plaque.

As long as you continue to experience the stressful situation, your brain continues to release the cortisones, which continue to make those tiny tears. The more tears, the more plaque. But the plaque can build up in the arteries, choking off the flow of blood. Deprive the brain of the blood it must have, and you suffer a stroke. Cut off blood from the heart, and you'll have a heart attack. To simplify a complicated chain of events, the body's reaction to prolonged exposure to a stressful situation can cause a stroke or a heart attack.

The Type-A Tiger and the Type-B Survivor

Some personality types seem to be more susceptible to stress than others. We call the most stress-prone among us "Type-A," and we've found that certain personality traits seem to go with the Type-A response. The classic Type-A tends to be argumentative and aggressive, for example. Type-A is rather inflexible in solving problems and constantly bounces from crisis to crisis. Type-A's like to call the shots.

The Type-A Tiger brings work home. Even when not working, Type-

A worries about work. To unwind, our Tiger likes to participate in competitive sports and to amass high-status possessions. Type-A may self-medicate with alcohol, Valium, or other drugs to try to relax at the end of a day spent revving the engines at full speed.

You'll have a tough time getting Type-A to take a vacation, and if you succeed, you may be sorry you did. Deprived of constant crises, Tigers tend to overstructure their leisure, racing from one "relaxing" recreation to the next and leaving themselves (and their companions) more tired than when the "rest" began.

Type-A's tend to suffer from burn-out, which can range from vague discontent to total emotional exhaustion and a sense of futility. And not surprisingly, given what we're learning about the relationship between stress and illness, Type-A's also get more than their share of ulcers, strokes and heart disease.

The Type-B Survivors feel a strong sense of commitment to work, but they can leave work at the office and become happily immersed in home and hobbies, friends and vacations. Type-B's tend to avoid alcohol and other drugs in favor of regular exercise, rest and a healthy diet. Whereas Type-A's may be rather humorless, Type-B's can laugh at their situation and at themselves.

And here's the real kicker: Type-B's tend to be more productive in the long run than the wheel-spinning Type-A's. By slowing down and achieving balance in their lives, the Survivors not only live happier, healthier lives, but they get more done as well.

Most experts now agree that to some extent these Type-A or Type-B behaviors are learned rather than inborn. Although it may not be easy, a Type-A can slide over at least partway on the scale toward a more relaxed, and ultimately more healthy and productive, way of life.

It's all in how you react to life's stressors. You'll never eliminate them, but you can learn to minimize their effect on you.

In the remaining chapters of Part III, we'll discuss the roles that rest and sleep, diet and exercise, and even just plain goofing off play in helping you minimize stress and live a happy and productive life. For now, let's explore how your mental attitude can help you handle your stress and even convert anxiety into positive energy.

How to relieve the stress—without drugs

By her own admission, Shirley Bender wasn't managing the stress in her life very well. She was trying to raise seven teenagers and get a small business going. Her marriage was shaky. When she began to suffer blindingly painful headaches, she started taking codeine two or three times a day.

Today Bender runs a successful glass business from her home in Appleton, Wisconsin. She also serves as president of I-ACT—the International Association of Clear Thinking—and she feels just fine, thank you. How'd she do it? Experts like Dr. Coe call it "cognitive adjustment." Bender just says she learned to change her way of thinking. After six weeks of studying stress-management techniques, Bender lost the headaches and the codeine.

Editor and writer Norman Cousins waged a public battle against stress. He was struck down by a spinal disease in 1964. Doctors said he'd be permanently paralyzed. Cousins didn't buy it. He figured if stress could make you sick, maybe love and laughter could make you well again.

His body knew how to heal itself, Cousins decided. He just needed to give it a chance. He radically changed his way of living, relying heavily on physical therapy and diet. He drew on family and friends for emotional support. And he watched a lot of funny movies—Laurel and Hardy, the Marx Brothers, anything that could make him laugh. Cousins laughed his way to recovery, confounding the experts.

When heart disease struck him down nineteen years later, doctors recommended bypass surgery. Let's wait, Cousins said. He again plunged into full-scale antistress therapy, and again he healed, without surgery.

Learning to give yourself a break

You don't have to wait until major illness forces you to make major life changes. You can learn to take care of yourself—physically, emotionally, spiritually—right now. Here are a few simple techniques to get you started.

Listen to your body

Your body knows what it needs, and it will tell you. But you must be sure to listen. Don't ignore signs of tension and fatigue. They're a call for help. Don't override the call for help with caffeine or alcohol. Listen and surrender.

Fifteen years ago, I developed what the doctor described as a "pre-ulcerous condition." It felt like a hot poker pressed against my guts in a spot about the size of a quarter just beneath the rib cage.

I eased back on the throttle, and the pain subsided. But for months after, every time I started to push myself too hard, my little ulcer spot would burn, warning me to stop and take a deep breath. I began to welcome the warning, and I eventually learned to pace myself without needing a pain in the gut as a reminder.

If you listen to the little signals—fatigue, dizziness, irritability—you won't force your body to provide broader hints—ulcers, strokes and heart attacks, which are surely nature's way of telling you to slow down. But make sure you decipher those little messages correctly. Most of us have a couple of peak energy periods and a couple of troughs every twenty-four hours, for example. When your body tells you it's hitting one of those troughs, you may mistake the message as a call for two glazed doughnuts and a large black coffee to go. In the short term, the sugar and caffeine will carry you through the lull. But you'll fall off the drug high and into a deeper trough. You'll need more doughnuts and coffee. The doughnuts will make you fat, and the coffee will make you wired. And you still won't have responded to the body's simple request for a little rest.

Likewise, a stiff shot of alcohol may seem like a great way to relax at the end of a tough day. But alcohol is a depressant, not a relaxant; it's a critical difference. Along with relaxed muscles (and inhibitions), alcohol can darken your attitude and disrupt the natural rest you really need. It carries empty calories into your body. And it can become psychologically and physically addictive. There are a lot safer and healthier ways to relax.

Give yourself a break

Replace the artificial and ineffectual boosters and relaxers with a genuine break: a brisk walk, some deep breathing, even a nap. Proper rest is so important to a happy, healthy and productive life, that we'll give it a whole chapter.

Talk back to the stressors

Jill Mork was devastated when her husband was killed in an accident. Out of necessity, she taught herself how to manage her stress, lessons that "saved my sanity," she says. Now Mork, a certified occupational therapist technician, teaches others how to talk back to stress.

Rather than serving as passive victim to your emotions and blaming others for your situation, take responsibility for your thoughts and feelings, Mork urges. The situation didn't make you angry; you let yourself get angry over it.

Instead of reacting, stop and decide how you want to react. You can break the event-emotion-reaction chain, she says, by thinking and evaluating before you react. Mork says it took her a year and a half to learn just this one technique and that she's able to respond in a healthy manner "about 92 or 93 percent of the time.

"I like the way I respond a whole lot better now," Mork says, and teaching others the technique is "the nicest gift I can give anybody."

Here's an example from the stress war zone. You're late for an appointment. You haven't allowed for the stop-and-go traffic. Some bozo cuts you off, making you slam on the brakes and miss the green light you were counting on making. The bozo sails through the signal and drives on.

You can feel the blood pounding in your head. You want to explode. Don't. You won't hurt the bozo, but you'll do yourself a lot of damage. Breathe. Short-circuit the anger. Ask yourself, "Is this worth hurting myself over?" Ask, "Do I want to give that bozo control over my life?" Put down the mental submachine gun.

Accept the situation. There'll always be a bozo. Remember, too, that you've been the bozo for others, cutting them off without even realizing it. It's part of the price we pay when so many of us live so close together and all try to get to the same place at the same time.

Owning it

Naming and taming the bozos in your life

We all have people in our lives who seem to have a gift for pushing the instant-angry button. The Rev. Ian Gregory, founder of the Polite Society, lists these among his top irritants:

- litterers
- aggressive and inattentive drivers
- surly clerks
- religious bigots (don't you just hate them?)
- untamed children

To Rev. Gregory's list, I would add folks who squat in the parking lot, waiting for a car to back out, so they can avoid having to park ten stalls farther away. And while I'm at it, I'd better include the folks in the parked cars who make the squatters—and everybody piled behind them—wait while they check their make-up, read their mail, write a novel, or whatever it is they do in there before they finally back out.

And what about the people who:

- talk loudly in movie theaters (especially when the talk has to do with what's about to happen in the movie)
- smoke in restaurants
- block the aisle with their grocery carts
- whip their kids in public (I suppose I'd be pretty upset by those who whip their kids in private, too, if I knew about them)

- abuse dogs, cats or other dependent critters
- tailgate

You'll never educate any of these bozos or "teach them a lesson" with words, hand gestures or other audiovisual aids. Any attempt to do so will simply result in your placement on the bozo's list of bozos. You can't change a bozo. But you can change your reaction. The next time somebody pushes your button, ask yourself, "Shall I let this bozo ruin my mood, my day, my health?" Ask it in an even bigger way: "Shall I let this bozo have dominion over me?"

When you put it that way, the answer seems pretty simple, doesn't it?

You don't have to get angry or frustrated. You don't have to let events control your mood. You don't have to be provoked by provocation. You don't have to get a knot in your intestine every time life derails your express. You don't have to wait for something good to happen to feel good. You can decide how you want to respond.

What to do when the road's congested, the receptionist never calls your name, and the guy ahead of you at the check-out has forty-two coupons and wants to pay in pennies

You must wait. The light will change to red. The receptionist will forget you're there. The line will be long, the checker slow.

You can curse and call it wasting time. Or you can relax and call it resting. Why not sit back and enjoy it? Life has just given you a chance to meditate, daydream, work a crossword puzzle, people-watch, eavesdrop, pluck the *National Enquirer* off the rack and read the headlines out loud—lots of little fun stuff you never take time for otherwise.

Instead of rushing through the day so you'll have time to rest, take the opportunities life gives you to rest along the way.

All your fuming won't make the line go faster anyway. (And yes, you do always pick the slowest line. In fact, the line, sensing your presence in it, actually slows down in response.) So why not stop fuming and surrender to the wait?

You'll still get angry. You'll still be impatient. Learning to declare peace on the world is the work of a lifetime. But you can reduce your stress response, and the more you practice, the better you'll get at it. As you do, you'll feel better, enjoy life more, and even get more done.

In our next three chapters, we'll develop ways to relax, to get our proper rest, and to change a frustrating wait into a short vacation.

CHAPTER NINE

Can you escape the tyranny of time?

"The world is too much with us, late and soon,
Getting and spending, we lay waste our powers."
WILLIAM WORDSWORTH

How to enter the Timeless Zone — anytime you want

Awareness of time is an ego trick, a way for Little Mind to call attention to itself and away from the task you're trying to carry out, the person you encounter, the world you experience. Keeping track of time calls you constantly back to awareness of the timekeeper, with its sense of its own importance and its pressing need to be somewhere else. Don't fall for the illusion. Don't abandon the vital, vivid present for the vague vapors of the future. Allow yourself to become engrossed in the now.

Losing yourself in the present
The Hopi language has many words for all the subtle shades of "now" but no word at all for "tomorrow." When I feel most pressured by the demands of time — how I envy the Hopi.

We met photojournalist Vern Arendt when we talked about right work in chapter seven. As staff photographer for the *Ozaukee Press* (Port Washington, Wisconsin), Arendt works long hours, often completing six or seven assignments in a day. He travels from one end of the county to the other, hard at it from early morning until long past sunset. Yet even for the most mundane assignments, his pictures are invariably interesting and evocative. His secret? Arendt's no Hopi, but he has developed his ability to immerse himself in the present, to suspend his sense of time and with it the urgent need to be someplace else, doing something else. He can lose himself in the moment, focusing completely on the task at hand.

Early in his career, Arendt's editor assigned him to photograph a pigeon in a bus depot. He didn't think much of the notion. He aspired to more significant subject matter. But he stayed open to the possibilities, took his time, and captured a shot of the pigeon standing in front of the men's room door, as if waiting his turn. That "dumb" assignment netted Arendt the first of many awards his photos have earned.

"Don't be thinking about the next assignment," Arendt says. "Finish the job you're doing."

Leaving the watch at home

The Bulova Watch Company once sponsored an experiment during which the citizens of North Conway, New Hampshire, went two days and two nights without any way of keeping time. According to the published accounts, some citizens reported becoming quite disoriented. A few even said they didn't know whether they were hungry because they didn't know if it was "meal time."

Would your stomach tell you when to eat? Would you eat when you got hungry, or would you check first to make sure it was "time to eat"? Perhaps you'd revert to body time and earth time instead of clock time.

Several experiments have placed humans in caves or other sealed environments, without access to time pieces or even sunlight. Most of the subjects established their own daily rhythms, although few conformed to a twenty-four-hour cycle.

Imagine yourself in a timeless environment. You might even go a day without a watch or clock — presumably not a day when you're scheduled to confer with the CEO or dine with the Queen.

A year without a watch

Along with his teaching duties, my colleague Harv Thompson directs a week-long summer program of the arts in northern Wisconsin and leads an annual tour of the theaters of England. He's a busy man. One morning, in his rush to get to work on time, he left his watch at home. He found himself glancing at his naked wrist often during the day and then checking a public timepiece when he needed to know what time it was.

As the day wore on, he became struck by how dependent he was on that little timekeeper he strapped to himself each day. He also realized that he didn't need to check the time as often as he had become accustomed to doing. The next morning he decided to leave the watch at home. He didn't check his wrist quite so often, and he got to all his appointments on time without the watch.

He left the watch off for almost a year. He learned to check the time less and to engage in the moment more. He was surprised to note that he was almost never late, though he didn't seem to worry about it as much.

Then one day he strapped the watch on again and has been wearing it ever since—but checking it less often than before his accidental plunge into timelessness.

I've gone watchless for several months. Like Thompson, I've found that a lot of time-checking is habitual, disrupts concentration, and ruins any chance of escaping into the Timeless Zone. I've also found that there are plenty of time reminders around when I need them. I don't know if I'll go back to wearing a watch, but for now, I think I'm doing better without it.

How many times a day do you glance at a watch or clock? Does time awareness destroy your concentration and lessen your ability to experience life in the moment? Only you can know. To test your time dependence, leave your watch at home tomorrow. At the end of the day, reflect on what you've learned from the experience.

Unscheduled trips to the Timeless Zone

Watch a reluctant schoolboy dawdling on his way to school. Watch that same schoolboy, free at the end of the day, fairly flying home to play. For that boy, an hour in the classroom seems to stretch on forever, while hours of play evaporate in an instant. We say that "time flies when you're having fun." It doesn't fly. It disappears. You cease being aware of it, and since you made it up in the first place, the moment you stop making it up, it no longer exists.

You escape time whenever you escape the realm of Word and enter the realm of Experience; whenever you escape self-conscious Little Mind and enter the Big Mind of impulse, image and instinct; whenever you escape Then and enter Now. You've taken many trips to the Timeless Zone, without planning to and perhaps without being aware of the excursion.

When you must spend time with someone who bores or irritates you, you remain constantly, painfully aware of the creepage of time. But time dissolves in your lover's eyes.

If you enjoy a movie, you don't ask, "How much longer?" In the darkened theater, the huge screen absorbs you, the sound track envelops you, and you lose yourself in the story. When you read a novel you love, you become unaware of turning the pages.

Watching a good movie or reading a good book makes you lose track of time. You forget that you're watching or reading, forget even that you exist. If the experience fails to transport you in this way—if you're constantly reminded of the contrivance of images or the assembly of words on paper—the movie or book has failed for you.

Former Stanford University and San Francisco 49er quarterback John Brodie has written about a strange sense of altered time perception world-class athletes sometimes dwell in. At times when he dropped back into the pocket formed by his blockers and searched for an open receiver to throw the ball to, Brodie writes, everyone seemed to move in slow motion. Brodie felt that he had infinite time to throw and then watch the ball spiral on its inevitable arc into the receiver's hands.

Although a major-league baseball player has less than a second to react to a ball being thrown at him at ninety miles an hour from just sixty feet, six inches away, the greatest hitters report that same sense of time slowing down, allowing them to react to the seams on the spinning ball, which tell them whether the ball will go straight or curve.

As a part of the vaunted "runner's high," that squirt of endorphin happy juice into the blood stream, joggers speak of losing themselves in the motion and forgetting about time, distance and pain.

Often I've had to fit the writing of this book into stolen scraps of time—the ninety minutes in the morning before the day's commerce begins, the forty-five minutes when I'm eating a sandwich at my computer instead of going out to lunch. But sometimes I've been able to sit down and write for long stretches, without the end time looming over me. Often during these gifts of time, I lose all track of time, lose the sense of myself writing, lose even the consciousness that I am making the words form on the screen. I seem to merge with the ideas and images the words are meant to express. I can't judge whether these passages are better than those I produce at other, less "inspired" times. I know that the writing is a joyful, exhilarating experience.

I've taken other trips to the Timeless Zone. Two that come to mind are so different for one another, they seem to defy generalization.

Trip number one: Walking on Balboa Island

While I was courting Ellen, we spent some time together on southern California's Balboa Island, just across the bay from Newport Beach. It's the sort of vacation spot where the fellow ambling down the street ahead of you might be a corporate lawyer, the owner of a major-league sports franchise or a movie star. Ellen's folks rented a home there for a couple of weeks each summer, and I was only too glad to come visit.

I remember one specific occasion, as Ellen and I sat out by the seawall, watching the sailboats slide by and the ferry lumber across the channel to the ocean side and back. We thought about going downtown to window shop or to ruin our dinner with one of the island's famous chocolate-covered bananas. But we just sat and talked, and the sun slid down the western sky into one of those endless southern California summer sunsets. Time was suspended in a twilight of grace.

Trip number two: Writing a novel in three days

One Labor Day weekend, I entered a novel-writing contest sponsored by a Canadian publisher. You had to write the whole novel in three days, beginning Saturday morning at 12:01 A.M. and working until midnight of Labor Day Monday.

It's a crazy thing to do and flies in the face of all notions of nurturing the creative impulse and letting stories develop at their own pace. But I figured I'd learn something about myself and my own creative process. And I suppose I harbored some hopes of winning the contest and having the novel published. (I didn't, and it wasn't.)

At a tick past midnight, I was off and typing, hammering away at what turned out to be a story about a boy from rural southeastern Wisconsin with an unusual gift. He could actually see the numbers appear on a scoreboard before the game had been played, a knack that his gambler father tried to take advantage of, with disastrous results. (Is that some terrific plot, or what?)

As I started writing, I was painfully aware of the passage of time, of my growing fatigue (I've never been able to take a preventive nap to store up sleep), of the still night and the noisy morning.

Panic mounted along with the pile of pages by the side of the typewriter. I was writing almost as quickly as I could type, without stopping or revising or even thinking much about where the story was going. But time seemed to be outdistancing me. How would I ever finish something worthy of being called a novel in just three days?

At some point Saturday evening, fatigue and the overwhelming silliness of what I was doing overcame my time fixation. I became absorbed in my story, began to live it, began to draw on the child with ESP inside of me and on the greedy manipulator and the nurturing mother and all the other characters who were also inside of me. I began to care only for the story, and then I stopped caring about it and just let it unfold. When I went upstairs for a stretch break, I was shocked to see how much time had passed without my being aware of it. I had lost all sense of time and self.

My timeless experience with Ellen at Balboa involved unpressured, unplanned drifting and total absorption in a human being with whom I was—and am—in love. My three days of forced labor in my little basement writing place involved intense pressure and focused effort. One experience was all about pleasure, the other all about work. Yet these experiences and all the other times I've spent in the Timeless Zone have these three characteristics in common:

- When I'm in the Timeless Zone, I'm absorbed in the moment. I don't dwell in the past or plan the future. I'm all here, all now.
- In the Timeless Zone, my concentration is intense but unforced.
- When I lose track of time, I also lose the nagging voice of Little Mind, with its "You should be's" and "Why aren't you's."

Planning a trip to the Timeless Zone — Why would you want to go?

Can you create such timeless interludes whenever you want? What would you gain if you could? I'll propose three reasons why you might want to plan a visit to the Timeless Zone.

Dropping the mask

Little Mind keeps track of time for you. That same timekeeper part of the conscious mind also stores a variety of rules, assumptions, limits and self-definitions. Little Mind applies the make-up for the face you present to the public, and it writes the scripts for your work and social interactions.

You need all that make-up and all those scripts to function in the roles you create and life thrusts on you. Little Mind makes sure you keep your appointments, get your work done, meet your social obligations, and avoid making untactful remarks or belching in public.

But there's more to you than the persona Little Mind creates. Just as George Reeves became typecast as television's Superman and could never land an important role again after the show went off the air, you can let yourself become typecast in your persona. You need to take off the mask, exercise other selves, think other thoughts, feel other feelings.

When you escape time, you also escape the mask. You can roam in Big Mind, where you've stored your dreams and fantasies, your doubts and fears, all your "unacceptable" urges. In Big Mind is wisdom, power and creativity beyond the limited imaginings of Little Mind.

Stopping to smell, look at, touch, and maybe even eat the roses

When I'm on the time treadmill, wearing my mask, reciting my lines, keeping to my schedule, I tend to wear blinders. I see only what I need to get the job done. You, too? Positive names for this characteristic include "focus" and "concentration." The more complex your world becomes, the more important this sort of concentration becomes.

But the itemized price tag for such single-minded concentration includes a long list of all the things you don't notice when you screen out everything you deem irrelevant or impractical. The negative words for this screening process include "tunnel vision" and "myopia."

You don't see, much less smell, the roses. You don't see the kitten in the window as you hurry down the street. You don't hear the melodies of the street musician. You might not even taste the lunch you're in such a hurry to eat so that you can get on to the next task on your to-do list.

You may miss the very images and ideas that would be most helpful to you in your work, your relationships, your attempts to understand life and your place in it. Chance comments, fleeting sensory impressions, the little story you happened upon while flipping idly through a magazine, could be precisely what you need.

Take some time each day to be totally where you are. See the kitten. Hear the melody. Take a nibble out of the nearest rose.

Making memories

Has anyone ever faced death with the firm assertion, "I just wish I'd spent more time at the office?"

When you think of the good times, the happy memories, what comes to mind? That big report you managed to finish on time? The day you checked everything off your "Priority-A" to-do list? I didn't think so.

My list of life's best moments includes some kissing and hugging, a canoe trip on Mirror Lake, an overnight in a cabin near Diamond Lake on the Continental Divide, a thunderstorm blowing in over the Yellowstone River, a sprinkling of Christmas mornings and surprise snowstorms, a warm montage of tail-wagging dogs and purring cats.

I spent all these times in the Timeless Zone. In memory I return to them for refreshment, solace and meaning, and they make all the other times of life make sense.

For these three reasons and for the many reasons you've probably thought of that are better than mine, finding access to the Timeless Zone is worth a little effort.

I'll share with you two examples of my efforts to dwell in that zone and the limited success I've had.

The loneliness—and pain—of the long-distance runner

Certain tribes of American Indians use long-distance running as a means of attaining spiritual purification. While running, they chant a sort of mantra that I roughly translate to mean, "I was born running. I will always be running. I will die running." As I understand it, the chant is a way to forget about where you're going and become absorbed in where you are. Be Here and Now rather than imagining yourself There and

Then, and you remove the anxiety and impatience about Getting Some-place.

I adopted this mantra for my own running, trying at the same time to impose a proper rhythm on my breathing. I wound up a breathless, sweaty wreck. In fatigue and despair, I gave up — and the rhythm found me. I found that I could at times achieve something akin to a trance. I was aware enough of my surroundings to keep to the path and avoid being hit by a car, but I was no longer aware of time or my own move-ment through it. In some way I don't pretend to understand, I had gained access to the Timeless Zone. I was no longer running; I *was* the running.

But despite all my chanting and breathing, pain could still disrupt the rhythm of the run and bring me back into time. I'd been jogging for twenty years, after all, and my body was showing the miles. I experi-enced knee pains, foot pains, side pains, lower back pains, even shoulder pains as I ran. I tried to ignore the pain, and it became more insistent.

So I made one more modification in my mental approach to running. Instead of ignoring the pain, I began focusing all my attention on it. When I concentrated on the pain, I felt warmth spreading through my body to the pain site. Within a few minutes, the pain would dissolve in the warmth.

I have no idea why or how this works. Perhaps it only works because I expect it to work, just as a placebo works because we believe that we are receiving help, thereby inducing the brain to release whatever chemical we need to ease pain, erase stress and heal injury.

This method works for me on the normal aches and pains of the road. It doesn't work on a bone spur, as I found out when I tried out my trance-running on a twenty-mile run from Madison to Stoughton, Wisconsin. I was putting in fifty to seventy miles a week of training, including a long run on Saturday. "Long" stretched from twelve to fif-teen and finally to eighteen miles. My mantras and breathing and pain-concentration worked beautifully, enabling me to find a loose, even rhythm and an almost effortless pace.

I looked forward to the race, confident that my training and my trance would see me through. A colleague who had participated the previous year assured me that the last few miles would be a "transcen-dent experience."

The last few miles were anything but transcendent. My trance de-serted me. Pain shot from my right foot all the way up my spine to my neck. I staggered through downtown Stoughton, crossed the finish line, sat down and never wanted to get up again.

When I was running alone on my familiar trails, I had no trouble escaping time and merging with the running. But with all those people lining the route and a timekeeper waiting at the end, I couldn't escape my self-conscious Little Mind. It's the difference between hitting home runs in batting practice and popping out during the game. And the pain of a bone spur on the heel was too great to send away.

I continue to meditate as I run, but I also go to the doctor when I'm not able to think away the pain.

On the road to Boston—and the Timeless Zone

When Jeremiah was still quite young and Ellen and I more reckless, we decided to drive straight through from Madison to visit my brother Dale in Boston for Thanksgiving. We lacked the means for air travel and the time for a leisurely drive. We had a relatively new car, we were young, we were tough, and we could split the driving. Also, our biological clocks operate in different time zones, so we figured we'd always have a fresh driver at the wheel.

I decided to see if my running mantra, slightly modified, would work on driving. "I was born driving," I chanted. "I will always be driving. I will die driving." Without body movement or endorphins flooding my system, it was hard to lose awareness of time, not to mention awareness of my aching shoulders and sore posterior. But with the help of the mantra and a gradual surrender to the Here and Now, I found my rhythm for nonstop driving. For long stretches of the road, I could forget about Get There and just Be Here.

I've used my mantra for other long drives since that marathon to Boston. It reminds me not to fight the present and instead to let go and let the motion carry me.

Owning it

Recalling your trips to the Timeless Zone

List occasions when you've lost track of time. Fill in details, being as specific as you can. Don't settle for "Reading a book." Probe for "sitting on a hillside, waiting for my car to be serviced, reading Earl Hamner's *The Homecoming* and becoming so absorbed, I got back to the auto shop after it had closed and had to walk home."

Spend time on this list. It will provide you with the basis for planning future trips to the Timeless Zone. After you've finished, sit for a few minutes, waiting to see if anything more comes to mind. Then set your list aside for a bit to let your less-conscious mind mull it over.

When you go back to take another look at your memories of the Timeless Zone, see if you can draw any conclusions about them. What do they have in common? What set of circumstances enabled you to escape from time? Can you duplicate those circumstances?

CHAPTER TEN

365 vacations a year

"[Our children's] life of play can save us from
working ourselves to death."
WAYNE OATES, *CONFESSIONS OF A WORKAHOLIC*

How to create daily rest and respite

The Timeless Zone may be a great place to visit, but the pressures of work and family won't allow you to live there even if you want to. Going into a trance won't get the day's work done or the responsibilities met.

You'll probably never be able to fully escape your schedule. So you must schedule your escape.

It doesn't take a trip to Tahiti or a sojourn to Shangri-la. You can take little vacations every day and return to your obligations revitalized. These breaks can make you whole again, even in a world that seems bent on breaking you into pieces.

The three-second time-out — The pause that really refreshes

An acquaintance of mine named Matt Joseph restores cars, writes for automotive specialty magazines, and conducts a popular car clinic originating on Wisconsin Public Radio. He drives a lot, testing out cars as well as getting from one obligation to the next. But even an expert like Joseph can learn an important lesson on the streets.

Joseph was negotiating downtown Madison traffic — we're no Boston or Dublin, but our town is developing some insane traffic patterns of its own — when he got cut off and nearly taken out by a rogue driver piloting what we Midwesterners refer to as a "beater" — a rusted-out hulk of a car, eroded by the salt we put on the roads to melt the ice.

Joseph figured the driver had no business being on the road and expressed his opinion with a few well-chosen words and gestures.

As Joseph pulled even with the miscreant at the next red light, the worthy in the next car drew a pistol and pointed it directly at Joseph's head!

He didn't shoot. Joseph didn't die. But he took the experience to heart. Now when somebody cuts him off in traffic, he takes a breath, quells his anger and drives on. You just never know when the fellow in the next car might be packing a rod.

You don't have to be a slave to your first reaction, be it anger, fear, humiliation or the giggling fits. You can decide how you'll react to the guy in the next car or to anybody else who crosses your path.

Give yourself time to make that choice. It only takes about three seconds. Take a breath. Bark. Blow air through your nose. Say, "Fiddle-de-dee, Melody" or "Winnemucca Wombats" five times, as fast as you can. Don't let those cortisones rip holes in your arteries. Think about how — or even if — you want to react. If you do that, you'll make the right decision — not the automatic rush to seek revenge or justice, but the self-enlightened decision to let go of what you can't change, to maintain a calm and positive attitude despite the crazy people and events around you.

If simply letting go of the anger seems too hard, visualize yourself mowing down your adversary with a machine gun (or whatever image suits you). Then take that deep, cleansing breath and let the image — along with the anger — go.

Even if the guy in the next car isn't packing a gun, why let him twist your guts into knots and send the adrenaline spurting through your system? Why give him any power over you at all?

The fifteen-second zone-out — Feeling the stress evaporate

Where does your stress live? Some get it right between the eyes, or even in the eyeball itself, in the form of a throbbing ache. For others, stress announces itself as a fiery fist in the gut or a sharp pain in the lower back. Stress knots my shoulder muscles and, if I leave them tensed long enough, migrates north into the base of my skull.

No matter where it goes, if you don't acknowledge and relieve your stress, it will surely settle in someplace. If you try to ignore the headache by popping a couple of aspirin and pushing on, the stress message may seize your attention with a louder announcement: heart attack, stroke or other debilitating disease.

Listen to your stress messages and respond to them. When you feel the tension build, take deep, slow breaths to replace the shallow panting a stressful day may have produced. Close your eyes and quiet the constant monkey-murmuring of Little Mind. If you're comfortable with it, engage in a little self-talk.

"Hey, shoulders," you might say. "I don't want you to be all knotty. You don't deserve that. You're very good shoulders. You've kept my head from rolling into my lap for all these years. None of this is your fault anyway. Relax."

Feel your shoulders drop as tension ebbs away, replaced by warmth. Your breathing slows. Your mind calms. Instead of frenzy, you'll feel a quiet surge of real power.

Don't even wait for the pain to start. Get in the habit of taking two or three zone-outs every day — deep breaths, a quieting of the mind, maybe a little comforting self-talk to replace the push-push-push, go-go-go message.

The fifteen-minute vacation — Getting away from it all without going anywhere

Before I describe this miniretreat for body, mind and soul, you must know that nobody will give you time, not fifteen minutes or even fifteen seconds, and not even for something as important as daily maintenance of your health and sanity. And you'll never *find* the time. You must *make* the time, and you may have to be fairly ruthless about it. Pressures, obligations, demands — scheduled and unscheduled — will never let up. Carve out a piece of precious time for yourself each day and use it to restore yourself.

I've found a number of ways to give myself a daily fifteen-minute vacation. Sometimes I walk to work, which obviously takes longer than biking or driving but which also provides an opportunity to get some good exercise. For fifteen minutes or so of that walk, I gently lead my mind away from planning the day and instead allow myself to observe everything around me: morning mist on the lake, the flock of ducks I startle into flight, the squirrel standing on its haunches, watching me with perfect concentration. Some of the landscape is less lovely: the trash strewn behind the fraternity houses, the algae scum on the lake in summer, the noise and fumes of the steady stream of automobiles on University Avenue. I pay attention to all of it, allowing my mind to relax and disengage.

Sometimes my vacation consists of a phoneless fifteen minutes at my desk with something good to read, but nothing from any "must read" list. If the phone rings, I let it ring. I pick a time when family members, students and clients aren't likely to want or need me.

Sometimes I just close my eyes and go away to a favorite place — a cabin on Columbine Lake, Colorado, where I spent parts of three summers; the miniature golf course at Lake Arrowhead Village, California;

the front porch swing of my boyhood home in Altadena, California, on a summer's evening, with a baseball game on the radio, and my father watering the lawn. Feelings of safety and contentment wash over and through me.

At other times, my vacation is a fifteen-minute duel with "The Ultimate Crossword Puzzle," a huge poster I've got taped to my office wall, with clues numbering 857 across and 851 down.

At home, I'll pick up my guitar and bang and howl my way through my repertoire of Roger Miller hits, ending up with a medley of spirituals including "Down by the Riverside," "Do Lord" and "Swing Low, Sweet Chariot." I'm no doubt inflicting great stress on anybody within earshot, but I'm doing wonders for my own stress levels.

Pick the activity—or lack of activity—that suits you, anything that helps you break the cycle of tension-on-tension that can leave you mentally and physically exhausted and even make you sick.

Taking a socially unacceptable siesta

We tend to look down on napping and nappers. Sleeping while the sun's up is okay for babies, old people and other weaklings, but a robust, hard-charging, gusto-grabbing American would never admit to needing a nap. So we've made sleep the ultimate deferred pleasure.

We also look down on those cultures that practice the midday rest. We call the siesta people "lazy." Maybe we ought to call them "smart."

We've had anecdotal evidence for years that some of our most productive thinkers (the likes of Thomas Edison) were nappers. Now comes a theory from Dr. Ernest L. Rossi, a clinical psychologist from Los Angeles, indicating that a couple of short naps each day, during the down times in what he calls our "ultradian rhythms," might reduce stress, maximize performance and improve health. Most of us don't take a break when we need one, he says, and we pay a price—physically, mentally and psychologically. Napping is restorative, Rossi says.

He's probably right, but I doubt I'll bring a mat to work and begin tucking myself in after lunch. I fought naps vigorously when I was a kid, as most kids do. I just never outgrew the feeling that I'd be missing something important while I napped. On those rare occasions when I've tried to sleep during daylight, I keep myself awake thinking of all the things I should and want to be doing.

But whether I take a nap is beside the point. Whether you get enough rest when you really need it, so you can function well and stay alert and cheerful, is precisely the point. A nap may be just what you need.

What a cat can teach us about napping

Cats are the champion nappers on earth.

I've kept cats all my adult life—a huge, lumbering tomcat named Spencer; a skittish black and white named Duffy; a totally eccentric half-Manx, half-Persian named Amanda; a sweet calico named Tuffy. I adopted a short-hair that I named Desdemona. For a while Ellen and I cared for her beautiful, long-haired cat named Fuzzy Kitty. We recently welcomed Ralph and Norton, full-blooded, nearly noseless Persians, into our happy home.

Each cat is different, but every cat I've ever known shared one trait: When they're tired, they sleep. They sleep on your pillow or your face, in the closet or in the middle of the living room floor, when the house is empty or when you're having a party. If they want a nap, they take a nap. If you try to interest them in chasing a string when they'd rather be napping, they scrunch their eyes tight and ignore you until you go away. Nothing on a cat's schedule is more important than the nap. If a cat made out a "to-do" list, almost all the A-1 priority items would be "take nap" (along with the occasional "eat kibble," "use box" and "scratch furniture").

For us it's the opposite. Rest is the last priority. We rob from rest to pay for work and pleasure. Cats rest when they feel like it. We rest when we finally allow ourselves to.

We have much to learn from the cat.

Learning to love the little everyday things

"The only healthy way to live is to learn to love all the little everyday things," according to Captain Augustus McCrae, the hero of Larry McMurtry's sprawling novel of the American west, *Lonesome Dove*.

Andy Rooney, the columnist and resident curmudgeon on "60 Minutes," wrote a marvelous column describing the everyday joy of a hot shower first thing in the morning, followed by the newspaper and the first cup of coffee. He wrote of loving to get to his work—something we've explored—and of loving to come home again. Don't wait for a life-threatening illness to teach you to appreciate such things, Rooney warned. Savor them each day.

I'm with Andy. We spend enough time mulling life's irritations. Let's focus on the good things of life. List a few of your favorite everyday miracles.

I love my morning newspapers and coffee and the conversation with my lifemate that often accompanies them. I love my Quaker Oat Squares for breakfast. I love my peanut butter, red onion, tomato and shredded carrot sandwich for lunch. I love some serious play with Rosie, the rogue

Schnauzer, and a little tag-team wrestling with Ralph and Norton, the Persian demolition squad. When I remember to appreciate these every-day miracles, they become a wonderful way to relieve tension and heighten my appreciation of the gift of life.

Taking note of the life-enhancers

While you're at it, list the pleasing people who help make life at least more bearable and often downright wonderful.

The other day I stopped in at my neighborhood branch bank—happily, this time, to make a deposit. I was lathered up from the bike ride, and I hadn't taken the time to make out the deposit slip ahead of time. So I sank into a chair, fished my checkbook out of my backpack, and set to my calculations.

Within seconds, a teller approached and politely asked if I needed help. She called me by name and gave me a fabulous smile. When I thanked her for her concern, she asked if I had a son named Jeremiah. I did, and how did you know to connect us? She made a rubbing motion from her cheekbones to her chin and said that we had the same facial structure along with the same last name.

Does she get paid to do that? No. She gets paid to take my checks and deposit slip, to make sure I've endorsed the former and calculated correctly on the latter, to process the transaction and give me my change, if any, and my receipt. Smiles are optional. Remembering names and deducing relationships are extraordinary.

The woman who holds down the information desk at the Wisconsin Center, where I teach my workshops when I'm in Madison, is another life-enhancer. With the room key and information, Jeanette always serves up a smile and words of encouragement. She makes my job easier and more fun.

Think back over the last week or so and note some of the things people did to, for and around you that delighted or uplifted you. What about the anonymous Good Samaritan who stopped and waved you into the line of traffic, saving you from a frustrating wait? Or the newspaper carrier who thoughtfully stuck the paper under the eave to protect it from the rain? Or the librarian who, noticing the common theme in the five books you were checking out, suggested another author you might also like? Or the clerk who called you back to give you the change you had left on the counter?

Such folks are out there, right alongside the horn-honkers and aisle-blockers. I'll bet they outnumber the pests, but we just don't notice them as much. The everyday courtesies may fail to register on us unless we make a point of noticing them.

Using carrots, sticks and two-by-fours

A lot of us use our simple pleasures as rewards for tasks accomplished. You probably learned to do so early on from messages you got from parents, teachers and other authorities. "As soon as you finish your homework, you can watch television." "No cookies before dinner. You'll spoil your appetite."

The gospel of delayed gratification can get fairly cosmic: Do the homework, get the grade, pass the course, graduate from the school, get the job—and *then* you can be happy. Spend the first twenty-one years of your life learning, the next forty-five or so working, and *then* you can retire and enjoy whatever's left of your life.

The time-management folks heartily endorse the carrot-and-stick approach, and the promise of reward surely seems to work a lot better than the threat of punishment as a motivational device.

But you might never get to the deferred reward. You can become too tired to enjoy the television show or the weekend or the retirement. The world could end, catching you with your mouth full of lima beans and that delicious lemon chiffon pie untouched in the refrigerator.

The reward can become a distraction. You might wind up thinking more about the peanut butter chocolate chip cookie you promised yourself after you finish the task than about the task itself.

The reward can become a substitute for the inherent value of the activity, as you could train yourself to do the work only as a way to get the reward and not for whatever the activity can teach you.

And all these wait-until-later messages might convince you that you don't deserve anything nice unless you perform first. That's a pretty sad message. You might never enjoy an accomplishment because you're too busy working toward the next one. You might even feel worthless and degraded, since you can never really earn or deserve the great gift of life in the first place.

I've tried to modify the reward-motivater technique in my own working life in two small ways, and I suggest you consider them.

Enjoy little rewards along the way
Don't wait until the end of the workday to give yourself a break. Take the three-second, fifteen-second and fifteen-minute retreats during the day, when you need and can most benefit from them.

Don't wait for retirement to take up fishing or to write the family history. Ease important pleasures into your life now.

Enjoy each task for its own sake
For a long time I wrote books that nobody published. I called these books "novels." Publishers called them "unmarketable." Then I began

writing magazine articles and getting many of them published. That felt good, a nice reward for my effort. I self-published a book on writing, and this is my third nonfiction book published by the good folks at Writer's Digest Books. Holding these books in my hand fills me with joy and satisfaction. It's a wonderful reward for all the labor. Receiving checks for the effort is also quite enjoyable.

But the reward comes a long, long time after the writing. If I didn't enjoy the writing, for its own sake and separate from any potential external reward, I doubt I could sustain the effort it requires.

I'm writing another novel, *The Year of the Buffalo*, about a minor-league baseball team in a fictitious Wisconsin town. It may get published, but it may also join the ranks of unpublished manuscripts sitting on the shelf in my basement. I'm writing the novel because I enjoy writing it. I also want to read it, and nobody else has written it yet.

I'm also writing the story of my father's life, something I'm finally emotionally ready to do, six years after his death. I anticipate a press run of perhaps twelve copies, for family members. Researching and writing the book are reward enough, giving me pleasure, satisfaction, and a rich sense of communion with my father. If family members enjoy and keep the book, that will be a bonus.

These tasks are thus self-rewarding. But what about those tedious chores you must do? Can you find value in finishing the algebra assignment, mopping the kitchen floor, attending the sales meeting, digging the ditch? What can you learn from these encounters? How can they help you grow? How can you enjoy being right where you are, doing exactly what you're doing? Many people expect you to dislike such tasks, just as they expect you to get mad at a discourteous driver. But you don't have to respond that way. You never have to do what "they" expect.

Shunning unrewarding rewards

Work doesn't have to be a pain. And rewards don't necessarily give pleasure.

You probably know more than one miserable retiree, people who walked away from productive and fulfilling jobs to pursue all the things they were supposed to want — sleeping late, golfing every day, catching up on all those classics gathering dust on the bookshelves or all those craft projects stuck away in the hall closet — only to find that all it took was a couple of weeks to get more than caught up on sleeping and golfing and knitting. For these poor idlers, even the activities that used to bring great pleasure aren't nearly as pleasurable as they were when they came at the end of a day or week or year of hard labor.

They may even secretly wish they were back at work, enjoying the camaraderie, solving the problems, meeting the challenges, and feeling productive and powerful instead of listless and useless. But retirement is supposed to be a reward for all those years of toil. What's the matter with these disgruntled loafers?

Nothing's the matter with them, except that they listened to conventional wisdom instead of to their own feelings and instincts.

It's the same with the woman who "rewards" herself for the week's work by spending Sunday afternoon roaming the shopping malls. She's supposed to love to shop, but her "malling" leaves her feeling exhausted, discontented and vaguely guilty. Her "fun" is just one more "supposed-to" tacked onto the list of obligations.

Everybody loves to party, right? Drinks, laughs, lots of chips and dip — what could be better after a hard week of having your nose rubbed raw on the grindstone? For some, probably nothing. But others hate parties, don't enjoy drinking, have a hard time dealing with people in herds, and would just as soon skip the dip.

Finding the right pleasures can be as elusive as finding the right work. For years I tried to make myself sleep late on weekends, because I'd gotten the clear message that I was supposed to want to. I didn't really want to at all. I was physically incapable of tricking my body into denying its natural rhythms, so I'd lie awake, my eyes firmly scrunched shut, while poor Ellen — who is decidedly not a morning person — heroically fought her way out of bed and took care of young Jeremiah. My weekend "reward" was actually a punishment for both of us.

Now I give myself the reward of getting up as early on Saturday and Sunday as I do during the week, getting in a good workout and savoring my coffee, my "Weekend Edition" on National Public Radio, and my newspapers. Dawn is my favorite time of day.

Can you think of any supposed pleasures that you really don't enjoy and would rather do without? List your rather-nots. Are there other things you'd rather do with that time? List the I'd-rathers. Can you begin to substitute items from the second list for items on the first, giving yourself real pleasures instead of false rewards? What's to stop you?

Owning it

Your personal R&R mission

Is proper rest an issue in your life? It is if:

- you find your energy and spirits seriously lagging during the day,
- you feel tension build as the day goes on,
- you have trouble relaxing when you finally get a chance to put your feet up at the end of the day.

You can change that. Examine your day, searching out opportunities for breaks, rewards and minivacations. If giving yourself a break doesn't come easily for you, if you feel guilty even thinking about it, don't trust yourself to rest when you need to. Schedule your breaks, and give those appointments to rest top-priority status.

Find the kind of break that does you the most good, and then take that break each workday for three weeks. It may become a welcome and integral part of your life pattern, and you won't be able to remember how you got through the day without it.

CHAPTER ELEVEN

Things that go wrong in the night

"When you are worried, and cannot sleep.
Just count your blessings, instead of sheep."
IRVING BERLIN, "COUNTING YOUR BLESSINGS"

How to get a good night's sleep

Perhaps no subject in our culture except sex is so studied, so talked about, and so misunderstood as the simple, natural act of sleeping.

As much as scientists have studied sleep in the last forty years, we still don't even know for sure why we need to sleep. Protein production actually decreases while we sleep, so the process doesn't seem to restore the body. And the brain doesn't rest. During dreaming, in fact, your brain is more active than when you're awake.

The clock-racers tell us we sleep too much. "Most people sleep themselves stupid," Arnold Bennett wrote back in 1910, and sleep expert Dr. Nathaniel Kleitzman informed *Saturday Evening Post* readers in 1957 that "very bright people need little sleep." (Wake up, you dummy!) But sleep experts now say we're a nation of sleep-deprived zombies.

Experts say that about 100 million Americans have trouble sleeping from time to time, and more than 30 million of us suffer from chronic sleeplessness. We're the only critters on earth who take drugs to put us to sleep and other drugs to wake us up again.

Why so many of us have trouble sleeping

The inability to sleep when or as much as you'd like is actually a symptom rather than a disease. Typically, we experience insomnia when we're under siege by a lot of stressors, such as loss of a job, end of a relationship, or death in the family.

Insomnia comes in two forms: *sleep-onset insomnia*, which is trouble falling asleep, and *sleep-maintenance insomnia*, which is trouble staying asleep. Both usually take care of themselves as soon as you remove the source of stress. But if you worry about not sleeping, you can prolong the problem. Experts call that a "positive feedback situation"—you tell yourself you won't sleep, and then you don't. They also call it "stupid." The worst thing you can do about not sleeping is to worry about not sleeping.

But you shouldn't ignore the stressors that may cause the insomnia. Therapist Mary Edwards reports that many of her clients who suffer with insomnia stay busy during the day to avoid dealing with a painful life situation. Insomnia, she says, is the body's way of saying, "Okay, so you won't deal with it during the day. Just see if you can go to sleep!"

Eventually, the body may "up the ante," Edwards says, creating sickness to force you to take time out and deal with the root problem.

Your lifestyle may create insomnia in other ways. For example, under one variant we'll call "college-student insomnia," you get used to staying up late and sleeping in late. But then conditions change (you graduate and get a job), and suddenly you're trying to get up early to an alarm clock. When you try going to bed earlier, you have trouble falling asleep. Again, this sort of problem usually works itself out after a few weeks, if you don't worry about it too much.

But worried or not, you're likely to experience problems sleeping if you get a job working the second or third shift. When you try to sleep while everybody else in the world is awake, you're courting "night-shift insomnia." It's just not easy to fool Mother Nature. Even if you can train yourself to sleep during the day, you'll throw your whole system off again the moment you get a day off and revert to more "normal" sleeping patterns.

If you use a lot of caffeine and nicotine, you may create "stimulant-induced insomnia." If you think that might be a problem, keep a sleep diary to record your patterns, particularly the amount of stimulants you consume. Most of us take in more than we realize. Once you cut down on the coffee and cigarettes, the sleep problem may disappear.

If stimulants are bad for sleep, you'd figure depressants such as alcohol would be good, right? No. Aside from its other potential dangers, alcohol disrupts natural sleep patterns. You may get to sleep rapidly after a few belts, but your sleep will be shallow and unrefreshing.

Other late-night horror shows

We bring most forms of insomnia on ourselves, and often a change in lifestyle or removal of a stressor will eliminate the problem. But some sleep problems are more serious and harder to deal with.

Everybody has a little *sleep apnea*, during which you stop breathing for a few seconds. For most of us, the episodes are short, infrequent and harmless. But some people stop breathing for fifteen seconds or longer, several times a night. Understandably, they tend to feel sluggish during the day and may even fall asleep inappropriately (while driving, for example), a condition known as *narcolepsy*. Someone watching you as you sleep can detect apnea. Generally, sleeping on your back tends to worsen apnea, and overweight people tend to suffer from the problem disproportionately. If it's a problem for you, get a referral to a sleep specialist.

Just as you drift off to sleep, you may suddenly jerk yourself awake, a condition known as the *startle reflex*. Again, most of us do it (I sometimes dream I'm falling out of a tree), but it's only a problem for a few. Some folks get the startle reflex hundreds of times a night. They, too, need a doctor's help. Medication can often ease the problem.

Some people physically act out their dreams, a condition known as *literal dream disorder*. If you dreamed you were snagging a long pass from Joe Montana and lugging it toward the goal line, you'd actually jump out of bed and carry the ball right into the bedroom dresser—or even out the bedroom window! Many literal dreamers and their bedmates wind up injured, and experts speculate that the disorder may even have caused some homicides. Again, there's medication that seems effective in dealing with this rare problem.

Literal dream disorder occurs primarily in older people, and in general we tend to have more problems sleeping as we age. This may be due to a general decline in health—more aches and pains to keep you awake. And sleep problems may gradually emerge because the body's natural rhythms become weaker as we get older.

To sleep, perchance to dream—Aye, there's the rub

Suppose you're in the middle of a sound sleep when suddenly your entire central nervous system goes haywire. Extreme physiological changes turn you as cold-blooded as a lizard. Your brain blocks out all external stimuli. If someone were to set off a bomb under your bed, you probably wouldn't even feel or hear it. Your brain then disables your motor system by shutting a little gate at the top of your spinal column, paralyzing you so that even if you did hear the bomb, you wouldn't be able to get up and run away.

Then your brain starts hallucinating, creating scenes ranging from fairly realistic depictions of everyday life to nonsensical dramas and horror movies.

In such a state, in the words of sleep expert Dr. Steven Weber, "all the physiological laws get thrown out the window." It is, Weber says, "a bizarre state of being."

Another exotic sleep disorder? Hardly. We call this state "dreaming," and you enter into it three or four times a night. You experience the vivid narratives we call dreams during REM (rapid eye movement) sleep. If you sleep eight hours, you'll probably have four REM periods, totaling about two hours, each period a bit longer than the preceding one. But you'll probably only remember twenty to thirty seconds' worth of a night's dreaming, so most of what you dream is lost in a process called *decoupling* of the dream from memory.

Most of us experience an occasional nightmare, and many of us suffer through anxiety dreams (you're late for the final exam you haven't studied for in a class you never bothered to attend, for example).

Some enter a state called *lucid dreaming*, in which the dreamers know they're dreaming and can actively change the dream or fight their way out of a bad dream. Some experts maintain that we can all be lucid dreamers by programming ourselves through presleep suggestion.

But all the suggestion in the world doesn't seem to help folks who suffer from *night terrors*, during which they scream and yell, sweat profusely and weep inconsolably. Such a performance is terrifying to watch, but the dreamer usually has no memory of the episode.

What — if anything — do dreams mean?

Dream literature has been around for about as long as language, and noted psychologist Carl Jung drew a lot of attention to dreams and their interpretation at the turn of the century. Most dream researchers agree that REM sleep is a natural and even necessary part of life, but they offer four basic theories of dreaming to choose from.

Dreams as psychic release or safety valve

According to Sigmund Freud, dreams are a safe way to vent antisocial impulses, such as sexual desire and violent aggression. You act out in dreams what your conscious mind forbids you to do — or even think about. Sleep researcher Dr. William Dement says that dreaming is your chance to go safely insane.

Dreams as window on the psyche

Jung and others have advanced the notion that dreams are a kind of therapy for working out emotional conflicts.

"Dreams are very meaningful," according to Mary Edwards; they provide a way for us to work out problems and prepare for the next step in our growth. "I trust that we're usually ready for whatever comes through in a dream," she says. "It may be painful, but not dangerous."

Edwards describes nightmares as "psychological shock therapy." We have nightmares for a reason, she says. She suggests keeping a dream journal to find the common themes so you can understand what your psyche tries to tell you. Rather than trying to control or "fix" the nightmare, which is only a symptom, you can then discover and deal with the true problem, Edwards says.

Pioneering sleep researcher Dr. Roz Cartwright holds that each night's series of dreams actually comprise a connected narrative, a sort of nocturnal novella. If you could remember the entire narrative, you would have a unified drama, with conflict and resolution, a mental mini-series.

Dreams as data processing system

A more mechanistic view holds that dreaming is a way of integrating life experience into the personality and of transferring learned material from short-term into long-term memory. This computer model of the brain views experience as bytes of information, dreams as a sort of data processing, using software we don't understand very well yet.

Dreams as random brain babble

At the opposite end of the spectrum from Freud, Jung and Edwards, many contemporary theorists hold that dreams have no particular significance at all, that they are simply the smoke from random mental firings of the synapses in the brain while you sleep. The higher-functioning part of the brain, the cerebral cortex, tries to make sense out of all that random internal stimuli by weaving the material into stories.

Many writers, artists, scientists and mathematicians have reported achieving insight and inspiration through dreams. Friedrich Kekulé had pursued the elusive molecular structure of the Benzine ring for years, for example, before falling asleep one night and dreaming of snakes biting their tails. Samuel Taylor Coleridge received "Kubla Khan" from one of the world's most famous dream stupors.

Whatever the reason for our dreams, they provide proof, if you need any, of each dreamer's remarkable imagination and creative power.

How much is enough—really?

A lot of folks say we don't get as much sleep as we should.

Some of us don't have a whole lot of choice. The single, working parent, for example, or the student working two jobs to get through school, has too much to do and not enough time to do it. Such folks have to get by on four or five hours of sleep, and they suffer for it with nervousness, irritability and decreased efficiency.

But a lot of us voluntarily deprive ourselves of sleep, for a variety of reasons, including:

- overstimulation
- the notion that not sleeping is "macho" or a sign of dedication
- the desire to get the edge while the competition is snoozing
- activities we'd rather do than sleep (such as watch David Letterman)
- habits detrimental to sleep

Are you getting enough sleep? Dr. Mark Chambers of the Stanford University Sleep Clinic says that the amount of sleep we need varies widely with the individual. Some of us can get by on as little as two or three hours a night, Chambers says, while others may need nine or ten hours on a regular basis. There's no such thing as "normal."

But Dr. Weber describes such talk as "the Thomas Edison myth" and maintains that even Edison got his six to eight hours a night. Weber will tell you the same thing your mother probably did: Most of us need around eight hours of sleep a night to be at our best.

Dream expert Maria von Fronz is said to average twelve hours of sleep a night. But then, she's actually working while she sleeps, so why not?

Although the experts don't agree on how much sleep is "normal" or even if there *is* a "normal," Chambers, Weber and others concur that many of us in this hurry-up Age of Anxiety cheat ourselves of sleep and are probably sleep-deprived to some extent. You can let your body tell you whether it's getting enough sleep. If you fall asleep during meetings and movies, you should probably try getting a little more sleep and see if the extra rest improves your mood and productivity. If you have trouble falling or staying asleep, you may be trying to force more sleep on yourself than you really need, perhaps simply because you aren't conforming to some notion of the "normal" amount.

If you decide to make a change in your sleep pattern, do so gradually. A sudden, zealous effort to go to sleep with the chickens instead of staying up until the bars close will almost certainly bring on sleeponset insomnia.

How can you get a good night's sleep?

You already know all the rules. Chances are if you follow them more faithfully, your sleep will improve. Here's what the experts tell us about improving the quality and quantity of your sleep, what Dr. Weber calls his "boring rules for healthy living":

Avoid nicotine, caffeine and alcohol
You keep hearing this from heart specialists, cancer specialists and now sleep doctors. There must be something to it.

Don't get hooked on sleeping pills
Don't try to self-medicate. Sleeping pills produce an artificial sleep, and you'll build up a tolerance to the drug and need bigger doses to achieve the same effect. Also, by "controlling" or "fixing" the symptom, as Edwards reminds us, you may cover up the true cause of your sleeplessness.

Keep regular meal times
That will help to regulate your internal clock.

Also, avoid pounding down the big meal too close to bedtime. Your body will get all involved in digestion and won't be able to relax and sleep.

Stick to regular bed and wake times, seven days a week
What, no staying up late Friday night and sleeping in on Saturday? Not if you want to reinforce a natural sleep cycle. You're better off going to bed and getting up at about the same time every day.

Exercise
People who exercise regularly tend to sleep more deeply than people who don't, and the exercisers also report a more restful sleep.

It doesn't have to be vigorous exercise, but take that walk, swim or whatever at a fairly predictable time each day. Avoid exercise within two hours of bedtime. It takes that long for the body to relax after a workout.

We'll look at some other benefits of regular exercise in the next chapter.

Don't worry about it
The occasional short night will do you no harm, but as we've seen, worrying about it might. If you can't sleep, get up and do something else until you feel tired. If worry is keeping you awake, try the "worry card" technique we explored earlier. Or you might really try "counting your blessings," as the song suggests.

A word to the "abnormal" sleeper

Earlier I told you I get up early each morning, seven mornings a week, Sundays and holidays included. But I didn't tell you how early. I didn't want you to think me a freak. Now that we know each other better, I'll confess. I usually get up around 5:00 A.M. (me, the dairy farmers and the newspaper carriers).

I exercise, write in my journal, read the newspapers, and have my bowl of oats with National Public Radio or the "Today" show. I shower and dress, and I'm ready to whip the world by about 7:30.

I usually fall asleep around 10:30 P.M., so I average about six and a half hours of sleep a night. Since I don't nap, that's usually it for each twenty-four-hour period.

That puts me outside the "normal" pattern, making me something of a sleep freak. But I know of many people with even more "deviant" patterns. A friend of mine wakes up at 3:30 A.M. and reads computer manuals for an hour or two (ugh) before going back to bed and sleeping until around 7:00.

Maybe you're a sleep freak, someone whose regular sleep pattern is markedly different from the norm. Perhaps you sleep four hours a night and feel fine. Perhaps you're asleep when the rest of us are awake and awake when the rest of us are sleeping. If so, and if you get along fine your way, then I have just two more suggestions for you:

1. Define what you do as "normal."
2. Keep doing it.

However, if you experience a dramatic change in your typical sleep pattern—sleeping much less or much more than usual—and you can't account for the disruption through any change in stress levels or life situation, be aware that sudden shifts in sleeping or eating habits often signal the onset of depression. You may need to talk to a doctor.

Owning it

A personal sleep assessment

If you're concerned that you're not getting your proper sleep, keep a sleep log for a few weeks. Note everything you eat, drink and smoke and when you eat, drink and smoke it. Also log any naps, planned or otherwise, and their length. Note what time you go to bed each night. In the morning, record how long it took you to get to sleep, how many times you awoke in the night and how long you slept.

Leave a space at the end of each twenty-four-hour cycle to comment on the quality of your sleep and your general sense of well-being the following day. Also note any outside factors that may have affected sleep, such as unusual stressors at work, the shock of a phone call in the still of the night, or the introduction of two Persian kittens into your sleeping environment.

Patterns will emerge. You'll know how long you sleep each night and how you feel about that sleep. You'll also understand how your habits may contribute to or get in the way of a good night's sleep.

If you're not satisfied with your sleep, compare your habits with those basic guidelines for healthy sleep we just went over. Introduce appropriate changes: less caffeine, more exercise, regular bedtimes.

Continue to keep your log, so you'll have a somewhat objective record for comparison rather than a subjective sense that things are better, worse or about the same. Continue with any change in habit for at least three weeks before making any decision about its effectiveness. If your new habits help to produce better sleep, without extracting too high a price elsewhere, keep reinforcing that new pattern until it becomes your normal way of doing things. If the change doesn't help, gently introduce another change, instead of or in addition to the first change.

If nothing seems to help and your sleep causes problems, talk to your general practitioner or internist and, if necessary, get a referral to a sleep specialist.

CHAPTER TWELVE

Will exercise and oat bran really help you live forever?

—or will they just give you bad knees and the runs?

Lose weight safely —
without dieting or painful exercise!
FITNESS, TELEVISION COMMERCIAL STYLE

How exercise and diet fit into your new slow-down lifestyle

In the first eleven chapters, we did a lot of resting. In the last chapter we even slept together, sort of. Now I'm going to try to roust you out of the sack and into motion. At the same time, I will suggest that you be careful about what you put into your mouth and how often you put it there.

Buddha, meet Richard Simmons.

You're of course free to skip this chapter. Your freedom to decide what you will do next is the most important lesson this book offers. More than anything, I want our time together to contribute to your sense of the possibilities in your life and your own power to choose from among those possibilities.

But I urge you not to flip ahead. I won't try to make you take up racquetball or compete in a triathlon. I have no intention of trying to make you forsake everything that tastes good in favor of something that looks like an eraser and tastes like it, too. (Yes, I'm talking tofu here.)

I also won't promise that working out regularly and eating oat bran three times a day will enable you to live forever or become immune to all illness. I won't even pretend that the suggestions I make here might not be contradicted tomorrow by some scientific study. As we noted earlier, "experts" used to assure us that eggs and bacon were part of the ideal breakfast. Next week, they may decide that tofu causes gingivitis.

But I will give you the best information we have so far, and I'll share those elements of my own experience that have had a positive and in some cases even a profound effect on my own physical, mental and emotional well-being.

Exercise and diet are important pieces of the puzzle. When you put all the pieces together, they'll create a picture of life as you really want to lead it, a life full of energy and vitality, productivity and joy.

The duel in the desert, the wimp-out in the weight room, and other embarrassments along the road to fitness

My development from couch slouch to energetic exerciser began amidst the cacti and sage outside Phoenix, Arizona. I was visiting my older brother, Dale, who was into jogging big time (he doesn't get into anything little time). I accepted his invitation to run with him one 115-degree afternoon. (Yeah, but it's *dry* heat, the natives will tell you, as if that made 115 not so hot.)

Dale had gotten better grades, but I had always fancied myself the athlete in our generation of Cook men. Sibling rivalry seized me. An evil intention overshadowed good sense. I'd show him what running was all about. I sprinted out and never looked back. Fighting off the agony messages my body desperately sent out, I circled the agreed-upon cactus and actually picked up the pace for the home stretch. As I did, every cigarette I'd ever smoked tried to back up on me. I beat my big brother, all right, and I lived to write about it, but just barely. I was dismayed at how bad a body still in its early twenties could feel.

Fast forward a couple of years. I'm married now, with a young son, in my first year of teaching at a community college in northern California. One afternoon I took a notion to pop up to Rockville Corners for a soda pop and, on a whim, decided to jog the half mile or so from my office.

I couldn't do it! After a hundred yards, I was sucking such serious wind I had to slow to a walk. I was shocked. At this rate of deterioration, I figured I'd soon need help getting in and out of the wheelchair.

I resolved to get "back into shape" (note the assumption that I had ever been in shape rather than simply younger). With the guidance of a colleague who had been jogging seriously for several years, I began plodding around a large field out behind campus (where few would see me). At first I could barely lap the field once. I finally built up to a mile, three times a week, and hit a plateau. Another spurt brought me to three miles per run.

And then I went a little nuts. Crazed by endorphins, the brain's home-brewed happy juice, I began running out among the orchards and vineyards surrounding the campus. I kept a mental mileage log, trying always to beat my previous daily and weekly records. One afternoon I ran all the way to the Wooden Valley Winery. I later drove the route and discovered that I had covered thirteen miles. I was hooked on big numbers.

My colleagues, Bob DaPrato and Bruce Clark ("Bobbo" and "Boomer"), had been giving me grief about my lack of upper-body development (which is to say, they kept calling me a "wimp"), so I finally started joining them in the weight room three times a week for what they euphemistically called a "workout." I added the weight training to my daily jog.

We discovered that the basketball court in the campus gym was often unoccupied about the time we finished lifting, so the three of us and a few students started playing a little half-court after weight-lifting. Again, I kept jogging. I had to keep up my mileage totals, didn't I?

I was getting home later and later, and all this good, healthy exercise was starting to kill me. I barely had enough energy to untie my running shoes. As she has so often done, my wife Ellen served as my voice of reason, asking the questions I should have been asking myself, such as, "Isn't exercise supposed to make you feel *better*?" and "Are you just going to keep adding things until you're working out all day?"

I blustered and huffed, defending the indefensible and justifying the unjustifiable. But slowly I began to seek moderation, a level of exercise that would keep me fit while providing me with energy for the rest of my living.

That was more than twenty years ago. I'm still jogging, although considerably less, having limped through bone spurs, pulled muscles and knee infections. I figure I've padded just about the equivalent of once around the world, and I've done it in twenty-seven states and two foreign countries.

I run about fifteen to twenty miles a week rather than the thirty-five to fifty I used to. I walk more and put in about forty-five miles a week on the bike-that-goes-nowhere in the basement. I continue to lift weights, but not so many at a time. I even shoot some hoops with my son on occasion, although the jump is pretty well gone from the jump shot.

I do all those things—but I don't do all of them every day.

Benefits of becoming a mover and shaker

Strange, isn't it? Many of us have been able to escape lives of hard physical labor, only to discover that all that sitting is doing us in, and we need to work movement back into our lives. If your life doesn't naturally include exercise, create natural exercise in your life. You'll look and feel better at least five ways.

You'll feel better physically

If you're just starting out, you must take this one on faith. For a while, you may feel pretty bad. Muscles that haven't moved since you were playing four-square and tree-tag won't respond well to a sudden wake-up call. But if you start slowly and stay with it, the pain will subside, and you'll begin toning instead of torturing.

You'll feel better mentally

You'll exercise more than just your muscles. Every time you forsake the couch for a workout, you'll release nature's own feel-good chemicals, endorphins.

You'll also send yourself some good messages about your own self-worth. When you exercise, you tell yourself that you're worth the effort. Any exercise of self-mastery in pursuit of a worthy goal brings with it feelings of well-being and confidence, which in turn motivate the next workout and the one after that.

The connection between exercise and improved mental outlook is well-established. Most of the therapies to treat depression now include exercise. Exercise alone may not be sufficient, but clearly, it seems to be necessary as part of a coordinated attack on treatable forms of depression.

You'll feel more energetic

Inactivity breeds more inactivity; yesterday's inertia makes it that much tougher to get up and go today. But once you break free of the gravitational pull of the couch, you'll find that activity also feeds on itself.

If you don't overdo it, exercise will boost your energy levels. You may feel tired after a workout, but you'll soon feel a surge of power and alertness that will carry you through the day.

Exercise will help you sleep better

We discussed that in the last chapter.

Exercise will help you attain and maintain an appropriate weight

If you want or need to lose weight, you must decrease the number of calories you take in and increase the number of calories you burn up. Dieting alone is a brutally difficult way to lose weight. Exercise helps because it burns calories.

If you diet without exercising, your body will tend to burn lean muscle tissue instead of fat. You may lose weight, but you'll actually hurt conditioning. If you fall off your diet and put the weight back on, you'll regain it in the form of fat. You'll wind up worse off than when you started.

Also, when you diet, your body thinks you just might be starving to death and adapts accordingly, lowering your metabolism to compensate for the decrease in calories. If you don't exercise, your body will fight your best efforts to lose weight. But if you *do* exercise, your metabolism stays high for several hours after you exercise. That means your furnace continues to burn more fuel even when you're back on the couch.

So how do you begin?

Carefully.

If it has been a while since you broke a serious sweat, get a physical exam to make sure all your systems are in good working order. My doctor, Mark Kaufman, knows a lot about diet and exercise and is himself in great condition, so I seek his advice about my own conditioning program.

Here are a few other guidelines for your workout program.

Commit for the long term

This isn't a thirty-day miracle crash course. You aren't "getting in shape" for some "season." You're committing to a new and better way of living. You're going to do this one day at a time and a little bit at a time. "Getting there" isn't half the fun—it's all "getting," and there is no "there."

If you must stop exercising for a while, because of interventions such as sickness, a week of nonstop meetings at work or a family crisis, don't despair and give up. Start in again, dropping back to a level that provides a satisfying workout without hurting you. Which brings us to—

Don't overdo

Slow and steady definitely wins this race. Some exercise, even just a little, is a great deal better than none. You may begin with nothing more than some slow stretches and a walk around the block. Your body will tell you if it's being tested or overtaxed. Build gradually, maintaining a level of exercise you can sustain without injury.

Do it regularly

Don't leave exercise open to debate. If you do, you'll lose. (We're infinitely clever at inventing reasons why we can't do things we know we should.) Schedule a regular time and place, and then just do it.

I've created many exercise patterns over the years. Right now, I exercise first thing in the morning, which:

* removes any worry about fitting it in later (actually, I'm often halfway through the workout before I become fully awake and realize what I'm doing to myself),
* burns a maximum amount of fat after the all-night fast,
* sets me up for the rest of the day with increased energy and a feeling of well-being.

A colleague, Bob Najem, swims during his lunch hour. Another, Lynn Entine, heads to the local mall for forty minutes of brisk walking after she drops the kids off at school. A third, Blake Kellogg, walks to and from work and takes his Labrador, "Budweiser," for a trek after work. Find the time that works best for you, with minimum disruption to family and work.

Avoid working out within an hour or two of bedtime, however. That roaring furnace can keep you awake.

What kind of exercise is right for you? Rowing machine, tummy-flattener and gym-in-a-box

I'm not sure we actually exercise all that much more these days, but we sure buy expensive shoes, color-coordinated outfits and fancy gadgets. You can buy a stationary bicycle that will take your pulse and blood pressure while it blows air in your face. You can buy a treadmill or a moving staircase. You can have your own "complete gym-in-a-box." (It looks suspiciously like an elastic cord with handles.) You can spend wads of money on special shoes that do everything but run the laps for you.

Jogging became the national religion. The prime way to bore people at parties shifted from the care and feeding of the wood-burning stove to runner's high. Then folks discovered that running tends to turn the knees into mush, the antijogging backlash hit, and walking became the rage. You may have assumed you knew how to walk—after all, you've been doing it for years—but books and magazines appeared overnight, promising to reveal the secrets of how to walk correctly. (It's all in the wrists and elbows.)

So what's the right kind of exercise for you?

If you hate it, you won't "just do it"; you'll just quit it. You'll then pronounce yourself an undisciplined failure and return to your slothful ways. So, find activities you can enjoy. Anything that sets your body into sustained motion —skating, skiing, shooting hoops, playing tennis, walking with Rover—all qualify. You can have fun, without buying any equipment or club memberships, and still receive all the other benefits.

Some folks like aerobic exercise classes or lap-swimming, both of which bore me to distraction. Some need the discipline of a scheduled time and place and a leader to put them through the paces; others thrive on solitary refinement. Vary your routine if that helps keep you motivated.

Where will you find the time?

You won't. As with every other good thing you try to add to your life, you must *make* the time.

I'm supposed to show you ways to save time, not spend more of it, and here I am suggesting more things to do. Saving time is a part of the bargain, all right. But the major premise here is that you can slow down, treat yourself better, even take a little time for yourself, experience a renewal of spirit and energy and still get all the "have-tos" and "want-tos" done with time to spare. Regular exercise is a key part of that plan.

Look for opportunities to build exercise into your life. If you normally spend thirty minutes reading the newspaper or watching the local news, you can ride a stationary bike while you keep current. Turn your daily minivacation into a brisk walk. Explore possibilities for biking or walking to work. If you must drive, park a bit farther away each week and walk in. Take the stairs instead of the elevator.

How much is enough?

If you feel good and are maintaining your target weight, you're probably doing enough.

The fitness gurus suggest that you get your heart rate elevated for a minimum of twenty minutes at a time, at least three times a week. To find your ideal heart rate, subtract your age from 220 and multiply the result by 0.75. If you're forty-seven, for example (to pick a number strictly at random), your target heart rate would be:

$$220 - 47 \times .75 = 129.75$$

or about 130 beats per minute.

But that's just an average. If your at-rest heartbeat is low to begin with, you'd have to work harder to drive it up to 130 than would someone with a relatively high normal rate.

Here's an easier way to figure out whether you're working hard enough to do any good. If you're not breathing hard, you're probably not working hard enough. But if you're breathing so hard you can't talk, you're probably working too hard.

Don't kill yourself. Ease into exercise. Pick something that's at least tolerable if not downright fun. You'll soon stop trying to figure out the minimum you can get away with and begin looking for ways to work different forms of exercise into your life every day. It becomes a healthy, happy habit, not a grudgingly performed duty.

Saying good-bye to Joe Camel, Jim Beam and other good-time pals

As I began to exercise, I had to forsake some of the friends of my youth. Cigarettes went early on. It just didn't make sense to smoke an unfiltered Camel cigarette before and after a vigorous workout. But I clung to my pipe and cigars for several more years.

When Ellen received a diagnosis of colon cancer several years ago, we were stunned. That sort of thing wasn't supposed to happen to young, healthy people like her. Fortunately, we caught the cancer before it spread, and she has been cancer-free ever since.

As a result, she has been on a high-fiber, low-fat regimen (she calls it the "tree bark and prunes" diet). My dietary conversion was somewhat less total; I still made occasional raids on Dotty Dumpling's Dowry, Madison's premier hamburger joint, and indulged in a bratwurst at the ball game. But since my dad and mom both contracted the same killer disease, I've gotten very friendly with falafel, and I eat so much oat bran, I should use a nose bag instead of a bowl.

Ellen and I jettisoned alcohol for a variety of reasons, some health-related, some having to do with the presence of alcoholism on both sides of the family and the difficulty in counseling our son to forsake booze while partaking ourselves.

I try to drink six to eight glasses of water a day, and I've kicked caffeine — several times. (I'm currently using.)

The stuff we used to feed to the pigs now qualifies as health food

Where we once thought eggs, red meat and whole milk were critical components of a healthy diet, we're now learning to cut down on animal fats and to eat grains, fresh fruits and vegetables. The much-maligned potato turns out to be one of nature's truly perfect foods. It's the butter and sour cream that can do you in.

I've interviewed cardiologists, oncologists, and specialists in sleep and stress. When it comes to diet, they all make the same recommendations:

1. Don't eat too much.

2. Eat more fiber.
3. Reduce the percentage of fat in your diet.

There are calories, and then there are calories. We tend to get 40 percent to 50 percent of our calories from fat, and doctors recommend we scale back to about 30 percent. Fats pack two to three times more calories per gram than do proteins or carbohydrates.

Now that many foods print the total number of calories and the number of grams of fat on the labels, you can run this quick test to determine the percentage of fat in that "nature bar" that claims to be so good for you. Multiply the number of grams of fat by nine to determine the number of calories contributed by fat. Divide that number by the total number of calories to get the percentage of calories from fat. For example, if that "health snack" has 220 calories and 12 grams of fat, you would figure the percentage of fat calories as follows:

12 grams of fat × 9 calories per fat gram = 108 calories
108 ÷ 220 total calories = 49.1 percent

or a pretty fatty mouthful for something supposedly good for you.

How to put your diet on a diet

This is a life-change, not a crash diet. You'll work to change long-term eating habits. You may need to learn new ways to plan and prepare meals, making low-fat substitutions wherever possible. For example:

- For whole milk, substitute skim. (Ellen and I got used to "blue milk" and now even prefer it.)
- For sour cream, substitute nonfat plain yogurt. (I was lucky; I don't particularly like sour cream. Ellen never has and never will get used to this substitute—but she eats it.)
- For ground beef, substitute ground turkey or lean ground beef. (Check the label to make sure "lean" is really "lean" in the meat as well as in the sales hype.)
- For breaded, fried fish, substitute the same fish, baked or broiled.

If going without pie seems too cruel, how about apple instead of pecan? How about vegetarian pizza instead of pepperoni with double cheese? Look for ways to keep both your fat intake and your feelings of martyrdom low.

Owning it

Creating your diet and exercise plan

You may need to make big changes, a few changes or no changes at all. If you're in any way dissatisfied with your weight, your overall physical well-being or your energy level, consider diet and exercise as areas for improvement. If necessary, keep a record of what you eat, how you exercise, and how often you exercise. Review a typical week's worth of information, comparing your habits with the suggestions we've explored in this chapter.

If you contemplate major changes in the way you eat and exercise, talk to your doctor first. Together, you may chart a course of gradual change.

You won't erase and replace old habits in a day or a week or a month. Creating your new life is the work of a lifetime. Listen to your body and make adjustments as you go.

CHAPTER THIRTEEN

Trivial pursuits

"The modern man thinks that everything
ought to be done for the sake of something
else, not for its own sake."
BERTRAND RUSSELL

Discovering the value in goofing off

"I don't have time to eat," a freelance writer/editor told me recently. "You can't bill a client while you're eating."

She had left the safe haven of the university and its predictable paycheck to become a full-time freelancer. She's a talented editor and print designer, and she does fine, but she lives with the constant knowledge that if she doesn't work, she doesn't earn.

A lawyer I know must account for his work time in fifteen-minute increments, so that he can build an accurate calculation of his "billable hours" for clients. In the highly competitive world of corporate law, he never would have made partner in his firm, he tells me, had he not put a high proportion of each day into the "billable" category.

Perhaps you work under that sort of time pressure. If so, I hope some of the suggestions you've encountered so far will help you deal with the stress that such pressure can produce. But in this chapter, I'm more concerned with the possibility that you might carry the notion of billable hours, or something akin to it, over into your off-office time.

The ancient Greeks held leisure to be our highest state, but America's Calvinist and Puritan founders passed laws against it. We've had a hard time dealing with leisure ever since. We define it as "nonwork," the absence of productive labor (just as we define peace as the absence of war).

We demand utilitarian value from every moment. Just try telling someone you're reading a book, taking a walk, listening to music or watching "Wheel of Fortune" just for the hell of it. Naw. You're improving your mind, getting your aerobic exercise, or relieving your stress.

How seriously we take even our play. Real fans don't just watch a football game, for example. They plan the week around it, turn it into a social event, gather information and develop strategies with the care and precision of military tacticians, bet money they can't afford to lose, root with quasi-religious fervor, become emotionally affected by the outcome of the game, and spend the week between games reviewing the previous game and previewing the upcoming one.

And those are people who just watch! Listen to some of those postgame interviews with the coaches and players to get a sense of how seriously the *participants* take their "game."

" 'Tis not the victory but the contest that delights," my dad liked to quote to me. But his was a minority view. In our culture, the game has no meaning without competition. Just try suggesting that you and your opponents not keep score the next time you go golfing or play bridge. Only victory validates the playing.

Taking the child out of childhood

We grudgingly allow for goofing off in only two stages of life: preschool and postwork.

Childhood probably represents the last stronghold of play for its own sake. But we've tried our best to take the fun out of it. Allow kids to choose sides, make up rules and play baseball by themselves all day? Never! We give them rules, uniforms, umpires, score books, statistics and standings. Unstructured time? Unthinkable. We shuttle kids from soccer practice to gymnastics lesson, exhausting them and ourselves. Boredom is the great enemy, so we fill the yawning chasm of unscheduled time with Meaningful, Purposeful Activity.

We even explain the spontaneous play we can't control in infants, talking about "developmental stages" and the importance of "floor time" (crawling) to the baby's progress. We worry that our kids don't goof off correctly, or that they might fall behind the other children in goofing off, might only goof off in the fiftieth percentile.

For a while there, the poor kids weren't even safe in the womb, but prebirth learning seems to have had its mercifully short vogue. I haven't heard about anybody playing Bach for their fetus or experimenting with in-vitro flash cards for several months now.

Child's play undoubtedly serves some developmental purpose, just as adult play does, but I'm not so sure we have a clue as to what that purpose is. Whatever the purpose we might assign it, that isn't why the kid plays. The kid plays because it's fun. Can't we let that be reason enough?

Structured or not, childhood gets over with in one huge hurry, as we older folk know. Soon it's time for school and twelve or fourteen or eighteen or more years of structured, evaluated learning, to prepare us for "life." But "life" turns out to be forty-five more years of structured, evaluated work. And when we're done with all the learning and the work, we receive a grace period called retirement in which to do whatever we want to do until we die. But after all those years of being told what to do, a lot of folks don't even remember what they wanted to do and wouldn't have enough energy to do it even if they did remember.

That's a crazy way to live. Doesn't it make a lot more sense to spread out throughout life the learning and the playing and the goofing off?

Defining "Iwanna" time

Let's look at leisure from another angle. Suppose you define leisure as "nonwork time," something to be filled with important, suspiciously worklike activity requiring schedules, priorities and measurable achievement. What would happen if you redefined it as "time to do exactly what you want" or "time to do or not do precisely as you please"?

If it's too hard to let go of definitions and associations of a word you're already familiar with, why not invent a new word? Let's call it "Iwanna" time. For "Iwanna" time, "I want to" is always reason enough—no redeeming social value necessary, no justification or explanation due, to yourself or to anybody else.

Have you ever asked the piano man to "Play it again, Sam," just because you wanted to hear the song again? (If not, don't worry. Bogart didn't actually say that line in *Casablanca*, either. Go ahead and check. It isn't there.) If you have, you were enjoying "Iwanna" time.

Have you ever gotten hooked on one of those pocket-sized video games, the kind that go bleep and blink and play happy little tunes when you score points? Just how do you justify such silliness? Sharpening your reflexes, you say? Relieving stress? Why not just put it in the "Iwanna" zone?

If that doesn't work for you (bless you, my fellow obsessive-compulsive), what about, "renewing the soul" or "letting the well refill"? Is that enough of a reason? We don't know for certain why we need to sleep, for example, but we know that in some way sleep renews us, mentally and physically, and if we don't sleep enough, we suffer. Maybe we need some "Iwanna" time for the same reason we need sleep.

Sometimes I sit and think . . . and sometimes I just sit

When I was in graduate school, my apartment mate, Kent Douglass (who has turned out to be a lifelong friend), spent a lot of time working crossword puzzles. I had not yet developed this particular addiction and so labeled it a "waste of time," which is simply to say I didn't understand why he did it. Fortunately, Kent didn't give a rap how I labeled his activities, which is as it should be.

Occasionally, I'd glance over at him from the kitchen table, where I was invariably pounding away on the typewriter, and catch him sitting on the sofa, a crossword puzzle in his lap, pencil in hand, mind apparently in another galaxy. Perhaps he was in the "Idonwanna" zone.

In case you wonder how this derelict ended up after all that sitting and staring, he got his degree, served in the Armed Forces, went to law school and is now a successful attorney, loving husband, father of two delightful daughters, pillar of church and community, passionate outdoorsman and friend of the earth.

And I'll bet he still sits and stares a bit.

To dream the impossible dream, to grow the ungrowable pumpkin, to grasp the unattainable mustard . . .

Dave Barry, perhaps our foremost chronicler of the inane and unnecessary, recently wrote a column on the World Pumpkin Confederation, a group dedicated to growing enormous pumpkins. (A recent issue of the confederation's newsletter contains an article on "fertilizing with bat guano," which seems to work quite well.)

Founder and president Ray Waterman has himself grown a pumpkin weighing more than six hundred pounds. The world-record pumpkin topped eight hundred pounds, and many pumpkin experts feel that the thousand-pound pumpkin may be within reach.

Ridiculous? Waste of time and energy? Well, sure. Not like, say, a good healthy obsession with mustard.

Barry Levenson was disconsolate. A lifelong Boston Red Sox fan, Levenson had suffered with his team for years. But even for a veteran like Levenson, the 1986 World Series was pretty tough to take, and after the final game, he found himself wandering the aisles of Woodman's Market on Madison's east side, looking for the meaning of life.

As fate would have it, he was in the condiments aisle when he found it.

"I realized I needed a hobby," he recalls.

He looked up from his brooding, and there, on the shelf before him, was mustard — plain mustard and fancy mustard, mild mustard and spicy mustard, good old American mustard and foreign mustard, mustard in glass bottles and mustard in plastic squeeze bottles.

"If you collect us," the mustard seemed to say to him, "they will come."

And so it began. Levenson started collecting and cataloging mustards of the world by night, maintaining his identity as a mild-mannered attorney amassing billable hours by day. At first he stored the mustards at home, but his hobby soon outgrew his house, so he moved his collection — by then consisting of sixty-five varieties of mustards — into a little building near his home in Mount Horeb, a community due west of Madison.

When folks started expressing an interest in seeing Levenson's one-of-a-kind collection, he created the world's first and only mustard museum. He started putting out a newsletter, *The Proper Mustard*, and realized that he could actually *sell* mustard — and mustard gift sets, mustard cookbooks, mustard T-shirts. . . .

But Levenson didn't start collecting mustard to make money. He started collecting mustard because it was there, and because it was a lot more reliable than the Boston Red Sox.

At last count, Levenson had 1,130 different mustards in his museum, which has outgrown its intimate, rustic little digs and is moving to Mount Horeb's Main Street.

The lady who hid the eggs

A Wisconsin artist named Sara Killian decided that she would make the world a brighter, better place with eggs — beautifully decorated eggs, an egg a day for an entire year. Just before Christmas a couple of years ago, she started hollowing out eggs, drawing, painting, and dying patterns on them, leaving them in different places around her hometown of Madison or whatever town she happened to be in. Each egg came with a note telling the finders that they could keep the eggs if they wanted them.

She wrote herself a note about leaving each egg and took a Polaroid picture or made a sketch of the egg, wherever she had hidden it.

Toward the end of her Year of the Egg, Killian invited 365 people from across the country to join the egg movement by creating one egg each and either putting it out for somebody to find or mailing it to someone they didn't know. She sent a blown egg to each participant, to decorate any way he or she wanted.

Lots of her "egg people" wrote to Killian and sent her pictures of their eggs. Many reported having had a hard time letting go of their little eggs and sending them out into the world. A lot of Killian's eggers found great meaning and joy in this simple act of creating and giving.

"I believe that the acts of remembering what we love and of acting on our own authority are powerful steps in a complex searching dance of change and reclamation," Killian wrote in a brochure describing her project. "My work is about searching out moves in this dance, basing my choreography upon my own experiences, questions and needs, always and never dancing alone."

That's what the project means to Killian. I suspect it means many things to the 365 people who found her eggs and decided to keep them. Surely it makes no sense, as the world judges. Does it make any sense to you? Must it make sense? Perhaps it makes joy instead.

Writing for something other than money

I write for a living, which means I write to make money. I've been told often enough that only a fool would write for any other reason. For a long time I believed it.

That kind of thinking made me fairly conservative in the projects I was willing to take on. If I couldn't see some sort of potential use for it—meaning the possibility of a market—I wasn't likely to try. I'm sure that kept me from trying a lot of projects that might have been fun, might have helped me to learn and grow, might even have translated into more of those dollars our society seems to equate with the very breath of life.

More and more, I've become the sort of fool who writes for reasons other than money.

I keep a journal because it's good for my head and my heart, but what I write in my journal is decidedly unpublishable.

I wrote a whole book for an audience of one, my son. On his eighteenth birthday, I presented him with *The Life and Times of Jeremy Cook*, a chronicle of his first eighteen years on earth.

I'm writing the story of my dad's life now. That one will have a much bigger press run, possibly all of twelve, for family members and friends.

I've been wrestling with a novel about minor league baseball—*The Year of the Buffalo*—for several years. No agent is putting heat on me to finish the manuscript, and Hollywood seems to struggle along without the film rights.

The funny part is, I find that the more chances I take with my writing, and the more relaxed I get about trying things out on paper, the more marketable ideas I develop and the better my career seems to go. There's certainly no guarantee that things will work out that way, but there's a simple enough explanation: Writing draws on creativity (as does everything else worth doing), and creativity requires risk-taking.

Owning it

Making time for a little goofing

Beginner's level

When's the last time you did something spontaneous, foolish, and totally without socially redeeming value?

Still thinking?

Get out your calendar, fellow scheduling junkie. Pick a time, any time, within the next week, and put a large "X" through about an hour's worth of otherwise unspoken-for time. You've just scheduled "Iwanna" time. Don't plan anything for that time. That's the point. When the time comes, stop whatever you're doing and do whatever you feel like.

If you don't feel like doing anything, or if you aren't sure what you feel like doing, don't do anything. If you've kept your whim locked up for years, doing nothing might be the toughest thing you've tried to do in years. Just sit until something better occurs to you. You need follow only one rule to make this experiment a success: Whatever you do, it can have no utilitarian value or purpose.

If all this spontaneity seems a little intimidating, go ahead and schedule a specific, pleasurable activity: a half hour of reading Sherlock Holmes before bedtime, for example. Then treat that appointment as seriously as any you keep all day.

Intermediate level

Let's suppose your 11:00 A.M. appointment cancels. Sure, you could attack the paperwork. Don't. Just once, take an unscheduled goof. "Pack up a picnic. Pick up a kayak," as Madison's local singing duo, Peter and Lou Berryman, suggest.

Leave no forwarding address, and do *not*, on pain of death, take a beeper or portable phone with you.

Advanced level

Take an unplanned goof instead of whatever you had planned. I don't advocate that you walk out of an important business meeting, fail to show up for the workshop you're supposed to lead, or leave your child waiting to be picked up at daycare. But a lot of our plans are on the schedule just because they're always on the schedule. Would the world end if you missed one of those highly missable meetings? Would the order of the universe be shaken if instead you took a walk, read a book by a river, wrote a letter to a friend, sketched a daisy, or thumbed through your baseball card collection, including your complete set of the 1957 World Champion Milwaukee Braves?

You'll never know until you try.

CHAPTER FOURTEEN

Spending time with books

"There is no Frigate like a Book
To take us Lands away."
EMILY DICKINSON

Slow down and savor the experience of others

The clock-racers don't talk much about reading, and when they do, it's usually to suggest that you learn to paw and claw the poor page, shake and rattle the meaning out of the book, without actually wasting time reading.

There's a place for speed reading as a way to get the gist of inter-office memos, annual reports, and even some self-help books (although not, of course, this one). A lot of this sort of writing doesn't merit or require reflection or lingering attention.

And you certainly don't want to slow yourself down by moving your lips, subvocalizing (repeating the words you're reading silently) or re-gressing (going back over material you've read and understood, simply out of habit or because you're insecure about reading).

But don't look for a primer on speed reading here. We're seeking the wisdom to be found in slowing down. There's a great deal to be said for regular, reflective reading, and we'll say it here.

Let's focus on books, rather than newspapers and magazines, because the book represents more of a commitment of time and effort (and thus deserves special attention in a book that's about slowing down for the truly important things in life).

Will the book survive the computer age?

I recently attended a lecture by a Dr. Patricia Carlson, delivered to an auditorium full of book lovers. She told us in no uncertain terms that the book is obsolete, soon to be replaced by interactive "text" on the computer. Instead of reading books, she said, we'll take "tours" of "knowledge space."

Printed text is rigid and unresponsive, she went on, whereas computer learning with something called "hypertext" is dynamic and responsive. Reading makes us passive recipients of information, whereas the computer allows us to be active.

For a fellow who writes books for a living, this wasn't good news. But vested interest aside, I don't buy Carlson's premise. With the advent of every new medium, folks have predicted the demise of the old. Radio was going to kill the newspaper. Television would slay radio and turn the movie theater into an indoor flea market. It doesn't happen that way. Old media adjust and adapt, finding a new niche, filling a new role.

And more important, I think Carlson's fundamental assumption about reading is flat-out wrong. The book readers I know aren't passive. They're seekers. They question what they read, comparing one source of information with another and integrating the information into their lives.

And how could you ever beat the book for convenience? You could never, for example, cozy up on the couch or sit under a tree by the lake with a good hypertext. You can carry a book with you and read it anywhere. You can check a book out of the library for free, and you don't need fifteen thousand dollars' worth of technological intervention to crack it. Books let you go at your own pace, let you linger or skip, fondle or fling. Most important, books don't just let you make mind pictures; they encourage it, even demand it of you.

I'd be impoverished without books. I don't want my text "hyper," thanks just the same. My friend and fellow bibliophile, Peter Gilmour, feels the same way. He writes,

> I come from the school of "always carry a book with you, always be in the midst of reading something." My greatest fear is being stuck in an elevator alone without a good book. I don't feel completely dressed lest I have a book with me. All this, for me, adds up, not to filling up every moment of my time, but realizing that there are many times during the day that are well-suited for reading.

He adds this cautionary note:

> I don't read all the time. Sometimes I just sit and think. Other

times I just sit. But many times the book I have with me saves these moments from frustration and unhappiness.

Reading as an active process

A book doesn't come to you; you must seek it out. Since there's so much to choose from, you must be selective. Once inside a book, you choose how much, how fast or slow, and for what reason. You make linkages, accept, question and reject. Even your retention is active and selective. If you're interested in what you read, you'll tend to remember it. If you're not interested but want to remember it anyway, you can increase your retention dramatically by previewing the material, jotting down a few questions, and then taking notes immediately after you read each section.

Unlike watching television or a movie or listening to the radio, you must learn how to read. You can certainly learn how to become a more selective and critical consumer of the electronic media, but only reading requires a fundamental ability to crack the code.

Reading takes effort. And like all the good things in life, it takes time, which brings us back to the premise for this book. When you cut out the time-wasters and the clutter in your life, one of the sweet things you've made room for is a good read.

Why we read

Some books are overtly inspirational or seek to help us live more meaningfully, even more spiritually (*Zen and the Art of* . . .). But wisdom is where you find it and where you create it, combining what you encounter with what you bring, the author's vision plus your own. Any book can be a wisdom book, if you get greater awareness of the human condition, greater insight into how you want to live, greater sensitivity to your world.

Reading for knowledge

I tend to gobble down nonfiction. I'm looking for information, not beautiful prose, rhythm or imagery. I pick and choose chapters and chunks of chapters, race through passages, read just the first sentences of paragraphs, pause to reflect on and note only a few.

Just now I'm reading about genealogy as I research my father's family to write his life story. I continue to read, skim and scan books on time, time management, stress, sleep, exercise and diet as I write this book. And I'm reading a lot about small towns in America for a project that may or may not come together into a book proposal but that fascinates me, whether anything comes of it or not.

I don't read these books because they're on some "must read" list. I read them because I want to know what's in them. My notes are nothing like the passive summaries I wrote while studying in school. Now I write only what I think is important to me, along with my interpretations, applications and reactions.

Reading for experience

Most books tell us stories. Fiction tells stories that never really happened (but nevertheless are true, if the author has been honest). Autobiography and biography are supposed to stick to fact but rely on narrative techniques. Most nonfiction uses anecdotes to illustrate points and to make the text more interesting.

All these stories constitute a kind of experience we call "vicarious" or secondhand, to distinguish it from events that actually happen to us. But Big Mind doesn't care about such distinctions. It takes the stories, real and imagined, from books and from life, and mixes them together to create new stories and new insights. In this process, secondhand experience is just as useful as the "real" stuff.

Reading for fun

Then there are those guilty little pleasures, the books you can't justify as sources of information, wisdom or experience, but are just a lot of fun. Some folks call this reading "escapist."

Humorist Dave Barry says he takes great pride in including nothing factual or accurate in his books. Maybe you'll find his wit socially significant (I think he's often right on the mark in pointing out the absurdities in the way we live), but maybe you won't. Who says you can't read him, or anybody else, just because he makes you laugh out loud?

Reading for beauty

We can never separate form from content, of course, but some reading provides a reward quite apart from any wisdom or experience it imparts. The writer must take time and effort to create such a reward, and the reader may have to take pains to claim it. But for those willing to slow down, the rhythm and sound of carefully crafted language may create intense pleasure and heightened awareness perhaps surpassed only by the creative process itself. A poem by William Stafford, a Christmas reflection by Truman Capote, a description by Toni Morrison beg the reader to pause, savor, and let the language roll off the lips and unfold in the mind.

Planning your reading or reading whatever comes into view

Louis L'Amour was one of our finest storytellers about the great American West. L'Amour not only spun a good yarn; he was a stickler for historically accurate detail. If he put a gun in a man's hand, you can be sure it was the kind of gun that man would have used in that place and at that time.

To make sure he got his facts straight, and to feed his enormous curiosity, L'Amour was a tireless researcher and an eclectic reader. He roamed through history, philosophy and religion, starting out as a young, uneducated wanderer who picked up and read whatever books he happened upon.

His way wasn't orderly, but L'Amour's marvelous mind absorbed, sifted and retained. He became one of our best examples of the self-educated scholar. He was a true intellectual, feeding his curiosity. It's no wonder he had so many stories to tell.

You can do it L'Amour's way. If you're interested in American literature, for example, go to the library, grab a foot and a half of fiction, sit down and start reading. If you find a writer you like, you can read everything she wrote.

Or you can get a map before you begin your book journey by:

- enrolling in an introductory class at the local two-year college or extension, thus letting an informed guide lead you
- checking out an introductory text, reading the sample bites and pursuing other works by the authors you like
- asking your reference librarian for recommendations

Traveling with a map will get you where you're going faster and minimize the danger of getting lost or stuck on a dead-end street. But you'll miss a lot of wonderful sideroads, and you'll rely on somebody else's perception of the terrain. Some American literature classes and texts, for example, stick to traditional and safe choices, leaving out anything remotely "experimental." Others omit women writers and writers of color.

My own reading has been a combination of directed study and rambling. I majored in English as an undergraduate, with a large dose of philosophy, a pretty good shot of history, and a smattering of the social sciences (and as little hard science and math as I could get away with). I loved Faulkner and Dostoevsky, struggled with Chaucer, was and am in awe of Shakespeare.

Since getting my master's in journalism in 1967, I've taken little formal course work but have read voraciously, trusting my judgment and following my instincts and inclinations.

Reflecting on what you read

I no longer have to "study" what I read, but I like to reflect on it, a process that helps me remember and truly own new experiences and ideas. This reflection takes three forms.

Often I'll read at night and then write about what I've read in my journal first thing the following morning. I note the main points as I remember them and play with the author's ideas. I try to be careful to keep the author's notions and my own separate, but I'm mostly interested in seeing what's new and interesting in the blend.

I often find myself mulling over the previous night's reading as I walk or bike to work. This mulling, as with the journal writing, helps to "set" new ideas in my mind and enables me to create new mixes.

I'm blessed with an intelligent, intellectually curious wife and colleagues like Blake Kellogg and Ellen Tyler. We discuss our reading, and their reactions further enrich the blend. In these ways, what I read becomes a part of me.

A few of the books that changed my life

The Secret Panel, a Hardy Boys mystery by Franklin W. Dixon (a pseudonym for Edward Stratemayer, who ran a fiction factory that also turned out the Nancy Drew series), got me started as a reader and was the first book I ever put my name in. *The Boy Scout Handbook* seemed able to teach me just about everything I needed to know. Later, the Bible served the same function. I encountered *Tom Sawyer*, *The Catcher in the Rye*, *To Kill a Mockingbird* and *Cat's Cradle* at just the right times in my development. These books shaped, motivated and inspired me. I can't imagine not having read them.

I've stored little bits of Ernest Hemingway's *The Old Man and the Sea* in my heart as well as my head. Hemingway could say so much with so few words. I guess he just stripped away everything that wasn't true.

I bought Harper Lee's *To Kill a Mockingbird* for twenty-five cents in hardback at a Friends of the Library sale at the Goodman Library, a beautiful old stone building in downtown Napa, California, precisely the sort of place where books ought to live. Lee gave me a hero in Atticus Finch and taught me that the writer's voice can seem simple while in fact being complex, as in the adult remembering the child's discovery and disillusionment.

Ellen introduced me to James Agee's *A Death in the Family* and taught me the value of rereading. Agee's image of Knoxville, Tennessee, in 1915, with the fathers all out watering their lawns after dinner, will be with me as long as I live.

With William Faulkner's *Light in August* I discovered that you don't always have to understand what you read to be profoundly moved by it. I went on to read all of Faulkner and couldn't think straight for months.

I got William Saroyan's *The Human Comedy* at a Napa book sale, too — paid a buck for it. My copy had belonged to Alice S. Moore. It won't change hands again until I die. Saroyan dared to write about the way we're all connected by our hearts, and he dared to write it with the directness and simplicity of a child. Reading Saroyan gives me hope and makes me brave.

Carson McCullers gives me the same kind of hope with her short story, "A Tree, a Rock, a Cloud," and her novel, *The Heart Is a Lonely Hunter*.

It seemed like a simple question: "Why are the Stamper brothers running that load of logs down the river?" But it took Ken Kesey several hundred pages of *Sometimes a Great Notion* and several generations of Stampers to answer, and even then, I still didn't know for sure. But what a feast of a story.

Afro-American Literature, edited by Hayden, Burrows and Lapides, introduced me to another culture and to gifted writers I might otherwise have missed: Jean Toomer, Langston Hughes, Richard Wright, Ralph Ellison, James Baldwin, Gwendolyn Brooks, Alice Walker, Claude McKay (whose mask analogy I used earlier in this book). I pursued many of these writers and have been greatly enriched for having done so.

I read Truman Capote's *A Christmas Memory* to my class every Christmas. Sometimes I cry, and sometimes I manage to keep the crying in. The descriptions are as beautiful and as right as any I've ever encountered, and Capote uses them to reveal truths of the human heart. "There's never two of anything." I will always see the dog, Queenie, looking up at the Christmas tree "in a trance of greed."

When I first read T.R. Pearson's *A Short History of a Small Place*, I felt the same way I did the first time I heard a Roger Miller song. Here's something new, way out there, wonderful. If you could combine William Faulkner and Garrison Keillor, you might get Pearson.

In *Lonesome Dove*, Larry McMurtry gave me words for what had been mute in my heart: We must learn to love the little everyday things. A wonderful story, with food for mind and soul.

William Least Heat Moon explored Chase County, Kansas, the land, the weather, the history, the towns and the people — more than six hundred packed pages called *PrairyErth* just for one little county in Kansas! Even the author admits it got out of hand, wound up three times longer than he had intended. And he says he had to leave out 99.99 percent. I've never known a place so well, never appreciated how much there is to know.

These books help me understand my power. They have given me new words and ideas to think with, new food for my hungry imagination.

I don't know who I'd be if I hadn't read these books, but I know I'd be somebody quite different.

Owning it

So many books, so little time

List a few books that have made a difference in your life. What do you remember from them? What did they teach you? How have they made you a different person?

List a few books you'd like to read—not because you think you should or because they're classics or because somebody told you you should or must, but because you feel drawn to them. Take a few weeks to let this list accumulate.

Circle the name of the book you'd like to start with. Go find that book and read it.

CHAPTER FIFTEEN

Discovering possibilities on the open road

"You can believe it if you read it in the Advertiser-Gleam. *"*
SLOGAN OF THE GUNTERSVILLE, ALABAMA, *ADVERTISER-GLEAM*

Letting the journey become the destination

Butch Miller tells the story of the time he hid in the nose of a Burlington Northern freight engine in the Lincoln, Nebraska, train yard. The train had stopped for a crew change, a perilous time for freight-hoppers like Miller, since yard detectives often take advantage of the stop to check the train for uninvited guests.

"I could hear footsteps coming up the stairs of our engine," he recalls of that tight squeeze in Lincoln. "If I got caught, I figured I'd get thrown off, maybe beaten up, maybe even taken to jail."

Miller says he looked through a peephole in the door and saw a figure appear in the cab of the engine. Within seconds, the door swung open, and Miller was looking down the wrong end of a .45 pistol.

Why would anybody knowingly put himself into that kind of danger? Miller says he's always been fascinated by trains. In the fourth grade, he made friends with the men who carried the mail on the trains, and they let him ride along and help sort. A few times, he got to ride in the engine and even operate the controls. He's been hooked ever since. Traveling on the upper deck of an auto rack or stowing away in a 3,500 horsepower freight engine is "true exhilaration, a natural high," he says.

A lot of us like to see our country from strange angles. If we don't hop the freight or meander on the blue highways ourselves, we like to read about the folks who do—Charles Kuralt (*On the Road With* . . .), John Steinbeck (*Travels With Charley*) and William Least Heat Moon (*Blue Highways*) prime among them.

I've read those books and dozens more, and I've spent hundreds of hours out on interstates, blue highways, and roads too small to register in any color on the map. Sometimes I've been on my way to someplace; sometimes I've just been on my way. In either case, I rarely take the straight line between two points.

From the point of view of the clock-racers, such meandering is a waste of time. Why spend days driving to California, when you can get there by plane in a few hours? But when I fly, I have the unsettling feeling that I haven't really gone anywhere, that they've just changed the set outside. The joy I discover out on the road enables me to come back to my "real world" and lead a fuller, more satisfying and ultimately more productive life. I need to take the time to break out, to explore the possibilities beyond my limited horizons. It's just another way to slow down and get more done.

I've driven alone and with various combinations of Ellen, Jeremiah, nieces, nephews and family pets. I've driven with each day's destination clearly marked off on the map and the night's lodging prearranged, and I've driven with whim as the navigator and nothing planned.

I'll share a few of my road encounters, a few of the lessons the road has taught me, and then invite you to embrace your own wanderlust.

Lessons only the road can teach

In my meanderings, I've learned that the smaller the town, the more grandiose the slogan on the town limits sign. I can give you a first-hand report on the demise of the drive-in movie. I can report that "service stations" have been replaced by minimarts with gas pumps, a boon if you need corn curls and soda pop, not so good if you've got a flat tire or an angry radiator. I can tell you that a lot of the folks who wait tables just don't care whether they get your order right. Having spent one night in Winslow, Arizona, and the next in Scottsdale, I can tell you that the gap between rich and poor in America has grown into a gulf bigger than the Grand Canyon.

But the real road lessons go deeper than generalizations about Life in America. When you head out onto the open road, you leave behind home, job, office, all your toys, habits, rituals and patterns. It's like stripping down to bare skin. Who are you, without all the things you own and do?

To some extent, you can impose your patterns on life on the road, of course—by eating only at the same franchise restaurants you have back home, for example. But even if you try hard, you won't be able to recreate home when you're out on the range. When you sit in an automobile for long hours, the thoughts and daydreams you didn't have time for back home finally catch up to you. New rhythms find you. You try out new behaviors. Shadow selves peek out, blink, and stretch in the sunshine. You take a new awareness of possibilities back to your "real life." You are changed by your journey.

Of sheep and geese

So much of the joy of the road comes from the unexpected, things that never make the guidebooks. I have a head and a heart full of these road memories.

Last summer, Ellen and I drove through the Big Horn Mountains into Sheridan, Wyoming. The map gave no warning of how steep the Big Horns are. We just kept going higher. Finally, as we crested the mountain, we saw a herd of sheep on the slope and, squatting on the hillside above the herd, a Basque sheepherder, staff in hand, keeping watch over the flock.

The image of the shepherd is, of course, central to the biblical account of the life of Jesus, and I've drawn on the image often in my life for guidance and inspiration. But I'd never seen a real shepherd before. I can picture him now, unmoving, his eyes on his flock. That image helped me understand shepherd in a deeper way. That understanding is an unexpected gift from the road, a grace bestowed on the traveler.

On another trip, Jeremiah and I camped at Goose Lake, on the California/Oregon border. We pitched our tent and prepared our meal in the lingering sunset and went to our sleeping bags early, having seen no evidence of how the lake had earned its name. I awoke in darkness, trying to figure out where I was and what I was hearing — an unearthly, unsettling cacophony that was of course the geese landing on the lake. There's no sensation quite like waking up in the blackness of the inside of a tent to a chorus of squawking geese. Another road grace.

The saint in the Chevy seed cap

Some of the wonderful surprises are only "wonderful" in the telling, as potential disaster turns into grace.

On one cross-country adventure, Jeremiah and I discovered that getting the Chevy started was a sometimes proposition — sometimes it started right up, sometimes it started on the fifth or eleventh try, sometimes you had to let it think things over before it would start. And one time it wouldn't start at all.

We had stopped for gas late in the afternoon at The Dalles Dam, Oregon, along the Columbia River. It's beautiful territory, with Mount Hood presiding over a series of magnificent peaks, but when the car refused to kick over, even after considerable meditation time, my son and I faced the prospect of "camping" in what I can only describe as a parking lot with water spigots that billed itself as a campgrounds. I was ready to drop my money into the honor box when a short, banty-legged man wearing a "Chevrolet" seed cap strutted up and greeted us with a cheerful, "How you fellas doin'?"

I allowed as how we were doin' fine but that our car wasn't so hot.

"That so?" he said. He squinted over at our sulking steed. "I worked on those things for forty years," he said. "Mind if I take a look?"

We didn't mind.

He lit up the requisite cigarette (who teaches mechanics how to dangle a two-inch cigarette ash over the engine of a car?), plunged his head under the hood and emitted a series of impressive grunts.

The smiling face emerged. "You fellas got a knife of some sort?"

He was going to operate, right there on the battlefield! Jeremiah got the knife we had been using to spread peanut butter on crackers. Our highway angel again disappeared under the hood.

"Go on and try to kick it over," he called out.

I got in under the wheel, pumped the gas and turned the key. The engine exploded into life. We were saved.

I don't remember the exact diagnosis. Something about a bald spot on the solenoid in the starter engine. (Does that make any sense?) By placing our knife on two bolts at the same time, we could bypass the problem and get the car started. We went on to a lovely state campground down the road that night and finished our trip, feeling utterly macho every time we worked our knife trick.

When the car died in Freemont, Nebraska, and wouldn't even respond to the trick, we had to resort to the ultimate tactic—calling a tow truck. As soon as the tow truck arrived, the engine kicked right over.

A head full of images

My road pictures are with me always, just below consciousness:

- gliding past the cows, passive in their pens outside Wazoo, Nebraska, and smelling the new rain on the pavement and the fields of corn alongside the road
- eating watermelon snow by Upper Clear Lake in the Paradise Valley of Montana
- staring down into the silent mystery of Crater Lake
- watching the dawn strike the red cliffs outside Sundance, Wyoming
- jogging on a rickety train trestle in Missoula, Montana

- peering up at Mount Rushmore and finding myself speechless with awe
- negotiating a sudden bend in the road and discovering a softball game, with what must have been most of the population of Sleepy Eye, Minnesota, either playing or watching

I've studied the American West, reading books and browsing museums. But after standing by the transplanted grave of Jeremiah "Mountain Man" Johnson outside Cody, Wyoming, and after inspecting the tombstones of Wild Bill Hickok and Calamity Jane on Mount Moriah, overlooking Deadwood, South Dakota, the West is much more real to me.

Local papers show you what's *really* going on

I buy the local newspapers wherever I go. Some of the bigger ones are full of wire-service news and syndicated features, and they're getting to be distressingly alike. But the little ones are still 100 percent local, quirky, reflective of the personality of the town and the editor.

By journalistic standards, some are a lot better than others, of course. But at their best—the *Advertiser-Gleam*, in Guntersville, Alabama; the *Index-Tribune* in Sonoma, California; the Vernon County *Broadcaster*, in Viroqua, Wisconsin; The *Rio Grande Sun* in Espanola, New Mexico—they are a weekly miracle of solid reporting, clear writing and courageous truth-telling, a journal of the way folks really live.

"Iraq seeks peace with Iran," the *New York Times* told the world on the front page of its August 16, 1990, edition. But the front page of the weekly Horicon, Wisconsin, *Reporter* passed on the Iraq story and featured instead the appointment of Alexendra E. Harvancik as the newest member of the Horicon police force, by unanimous vote of the city council. The *Daily Citizen* in Beaver Dam went with the crowning of an Iron Ridge woman as the 1990 Miss Dodge County Fair. The banner headline on its lead story for the August 16 edition of the Kiel, Wisconsin, *Tri-County Record* proclaimed, "Students return to school August 30." No mention of Iraq in the whole paper, but a big picture of the llamas participating in the 1990 Kiel Parade made page one.

Was editor Mike Mathes sleeping through the whole Iraq mess? No, Mathes didn't miss the story. He just didn't run it. Like any good community newspaper editor (and he's a darn good one), Mathes covers Kiel as nobody else can or will.

From reading the *Advertiser-Gleam*, I learned about the tomcat with no tail, belonging to Greg and Leanne Willis; about the twenty-seven-pound cantaloupe that Harvie Collins grew from seed; about Fred and Vera Nell Walden's duck that thinks it's a chicken; about E. B. Barfield Sr.'s miraculous light bulb, that finally burned out after twenty-one years; about the day in February, 1987, when Jackie Till got dealt thirteen hearts at the weekly bridge game at Reid's Restaurant, and came up second best to Helen Howell's thirteen spades. (Annie Mae Grant held thirteen diamonds, and Lee McCoy thirteen clubs.) The editors say the odds of that happening are "trillions and trillions to one," and I read about it in the *Gleam*.

In the small-town paper, even "dog bites man" makes news (*Advertiser-Gleam*, April 6, 1988).

Take me out to the ballyard

Like the local newspaper, the local baseball park tells a lot about the people and the town you're in. I'm not talking major league, not on the highways I travel. I'm talking Pioneer League, Rookie League, Class A, American Legion. The parks are all the same, yet each one is different.

Pilot Stadium in Buffalo, New York, and Cashman Field in Las Vegas, Nevada, are modern, spiffy parks with fancy restaurants. Sam Lynn Ball Park in Bakersfield, California, is a funky old falling-down stockade.

Lawrence-Dumont Stadium is right in the heart of Wichita, Kansas. Sports Stadium sits up on a hill, far removed from downtown Albuquerque, New Mexico.

Early season games just might get snowed out in Madison, Wisconsin, my hometown. But they use baseball's only "cool mist" water spray to keep the fans comfortable in Phoenix's sweltering Municipal Stadium.

The huge Marlboro Man, saddle slung over his shoulder, still broods over the outfield in a lot of the older parks, but the newer parks have those fancy electronic scoreboards, many bearing the logos of the beer companies that donated them.

But no matter what shape the park is in, inside every park, big and small, old and new, the crowd forms a community—adolescents parading in packs, young couples holding hands and draping their arms possessively over each other, parents keeping loose tabs on herds of little kids. The stands are constant motion, like a campground just before supper time.

You'll find nachos and beer and little batting helmets filled with soft ice cream, along with the peanuts and popcorn and Cracker Jack, almost everywhere. But lots of parks have their own special foods. You ought to sample the Monroe Street chili stew in Albuquerque.

Most of the public address announcers get all excited announcing the home-team heroes, stretching the names out for thirteen or fourteen extra syllables. And a lot of them use the venerable shattering glass sound effect for foul balls hit into the parking lot. But there are wonderful local variations on the theme. In Phoenix, they play the Looney Tunes theme when an opposing player screws up, and in Wichita, if the announcer thinks the home team got a raw deal on the ump's call, he just might play Linda Ronstadt's "When Will I Be Loved?" ("I've been cheated, been mistreated").

Lots of teams still have their mascots: Wichita its Wrangler; Madison its Mike the Muskie; Bakersfield its Roger the Dodger, a low-rent version of the Phillie Phanatic.

But none of that fully explains the magic. Ask me why I love the local ball park, and I could list all those facts for you, but they wouldn't add up to love. Sitting in Denton Field, watching the Miles City, Montana, American Legion team beat up on visiting Glendive — with no mascots or Linda Ronstadt or other frills, just a few of us in the stands and about the same number performing the rituals down on the field, I'm as happy as I'd be in any park anywhere.

Doughnuts the size of life preservers

When you're on the road, you're at the mercy of road food. The quest for edible fare can be frustrating, especially if you're trying to stick to the tree bark and prunes diet.

Most towns of any size at all have their McDonald's and the like now. You can get a perfectly decent salad at McDonald's, a recent concession to our growing nutritional awareness. And that perfectly decent McDonald's salad will be exactly like every other perfectly decent McDonald's salad in every other town in the world. That's a comfort.

But I like to take my chances sometimes. I don't think a McAnything could top the one-of-a-kind breakfast at the family restaurant in Greensburg, Kansas, "Home of the deepest hand-dug well in America," for example. I had canned peaches and eggs over, done just right. The folks at the next table wore spurs. The waitress had time to stop and chat while she refilled our coffee mugs.

I've suffered through some pretty bad meals, too, of course. But I've encountered such wonderful surprises, like the breakfast Ellen, Jeremiah and I had at Donna's Diner, Battle Mountain, Nevada, several years ago. Everything was homemade and delicious, including doughnuts the size of life preservers and the finest browned-on-the-outside, moist-on-the-inside, flaky, greasy miracle hashbrowns I've ever had.

Life in Vega, along the old Route 66

They may call it "Business 40" now, but the folks in Vega, Texas, know they live on the old Route 66.

Plumber Edward Murphy keeps the memory and legend of the old Route 66 alive in Vega by publishing the quarterly *Oldham County News*, a scrapbook of old photos, wit and wisdom. An implements dealer on the east side of town has left up the "Route 66 Cafe" sign, and you can buy your Route 66 T-shirts and postcards at the fine cafe adjacent to the Sands Best Western Motel on the western edge of town.

Vega, population nine hundred, seat of Oldham County, in the west Texas panhandle, is home to the Vega High School Longhorns, and they let you know it all over town. A longhorn steer peers down from the water tower and the grain silo and from many store windows, and each year the new herd of cheerleaders stencils the image all along Longhorn Drive, leading to the school. The Longhorns are the biggest show in town, and the high school is the focal point in the community.

Imogene Galbraith edits and publishes the weekly *Vega Enterprise* — weekly, that is, except one week at Christmastime, and reports on all the Longhorn doings. The *Enterprise* is a friendly four-pager that carries school menus, a column from one of the local ministers and the front page "Sheriff's Communique," which recently included a report on the break-in at the Catholic church and "a large amount of criminal mischief and destruction."

Despite this crimewave, folks are friendly here, waving to strangers and taking time to chat if you care to.

The library down on the courthouse square is open every other afternoon from 12:00 to 6:00 and offers a clean, comfortable place to browse, with a special section marked off and decorated for kids. It's the only library in the county, and determined locals had to battle public resistance all the way to court to get it going in 1987. When we visited, librarian Gayna Stephenson was selling hardbound books for a quarter because they had more books than they had shelf space. (We bought a trunkful.)

"At first, a lot of folks wouldn't have been caught dead coming in here," Stephenson says. "But they're coming around now."

Every tree on the courthouse lawn had a yellow ribbon tied to it, and each ribbon carried the name of a local man or woman serving in the Persian Gulf.

Signs in the window at the grocery announced the forty-third annual Oldham County Roundup, coming up in a few days, with a parade, team roping, free barbecue and music.

Greg Pollard was running the local Shell Station when we pulled in for a fill-up on our way out of town. Greg told us he'd tried the big cities, and he likes Vega the best.

Whenever I visit a town like Vega, I think about what it would be like to live there. In some ways, life would be much the same. I could still read the headlines out of the *National Enquirer* at the checkout counter in the market, I could still choose to watch or not watch "Roseanne" on the television, and I could still have my Cracklin' Oat Bran and Quaker Oat Squares for breakfast.

But what differences, starting with about 171,000 fewer people than in Madison, and not a lake or dairy cow in sight.

Trying on different lives in different places is a safe way to explore the possibilities of life. The fantasy enriches my life by suggesting variations on that life and by allowing me to exercise some of my shadow selves.

Back in the saddle again

Whenever I come home from a long road trip, I feel the road for several days afterward. When I close my eyes at night, I see the center line of the highway, and I feel the motion of the car. My dreams are full of the places I've seen.

But it's so nice to be home again! All the familiar objects seem so dear, and I reclaim simple pleasures, reembrace old routines, made new by absence and somehow changed by all I've seen and experienced, because I've changed.

And I don't even feel like hitting the road again for, oh, several weeks.

Owning it

Putting yourself in a new place

Recall the place you've visited that is the least like the place where you live. Bring it to mind as vividly as you can, filling in specific details, and then think about these questions: How is this place different from home? How is it the same? What would it be like to live there? What would I be like if I lived there? How might my awareness of this place change the way I live?

You can ask these questions about places you've "visited" in books, movies and television shows, too. I've visited the "Cicely, Alaska" of *Northern Exposure* and David Lynch's spooky *Twin Peaks* as surely as I've visited Vega, Texas. Imagination need never be bounded by "reality" or narrow definitions of "truth."

Some other questions to set you on a little mental journey:

- What does my ideal city, town or village look like?
- How is it different from the place I live?
- How can I make my real place more like my ideal place?
- How much of the ideal is "out there," and how much can I create in the way I think and live right where I am?

CHAPTER SIXTEEN

Running naked in the streets

We can't not think, not get ideas.
Something always occurs.
WILLIAM STAFFORD, *A WAY OF WRITING*

How to slow down and become constantly creative

"I'm just not very creative."

Have you caught yourself thinking that? It isn't true. You have almost infinite capacity for inventiveness and creativity. But when you get caught in the time trap, hurrying from place to place and item to item on the "must-do" list, you leave no time for the reflection, the simmering, and the incubation that yield the flashes of insight we call creativity.

Creativity is discovery. It involves gathering and joining ideas nobody put together before. It's the triumph of originality over habit. If you would create, you must remain flexible and receptive. You must pay profound attention to the world within *and* the world without.

Sometimes you must wait. Creativity keeps its own schedule. You seek an answer for days and finally give up; the answer finds you in the night. You shout your question; your answer comes in the silence.

Creativity is sometimes messy and often inconvenient.

Discovering an idea is a little like drilling for oil. You have reason to believe there's oil down there someplace. You drill. You wait and hope. You may have to sink a lot of shafts, endure a lot of dry wells. The payoff is a great, joyful gusher, surpassing anything you dared to imagine.

Creativity is a lot of hard work, and it's the most joyful play
there is.

Creativity is: allowing, accepting, nurturing, tolerating, forgiv-
ing, risking.

Creativity is not: judging, evaluating, competing, rebuking, cor-
recting.

Creativity is: Let's try and see what happens.

Creativity is not: We must find the right answer.

The seeker asks, "How do you get ideas?"

Creativity responds, "You will never stop getting them."

The secret of creative thinking revealed — Put a lot of bees in your mental meadow

Creativity is a joyful eruption, an excitement, two ideas from different
worlds fusing into a third idea, different from anything the two original
ideas would seem to be able to produce. This fusion ignites a fire, and
the fire illuminates your world.

Archimedes was taking his daily bath when the theory of displace-
ment ignited in his mind; he got so excited, legend has it, he jumped
up, shouted "Eureka!" and ran out into the streets — without bothering
to put his clothes on. You may not react as Archimedes did. You may
simply feel a wave of wonder and gratitude. Whatever the feeling, it will
be good. Take the time to appreciate and enjoy it, thereby encouraging
the next fusion, the next creative illumination.

The more ideas you collect, the more fusions you create. Imagine a
vast meadow with but one bee and one flower. Odds are the bee will
buzz around for a long time before it finds the flower. And even when
it does, there will be no second flower for it to pollinate. But populate
this vast mental meadow with thousands of bees and thousands of flowers. Suddenly, you've got a whole lot of pollination going on.

Your creativity is like that vast meadow. Experiences and information are your bees and your flowers. If you want a lot of pollination, a
lot of creative unions, you must fill your mind with experience and
information. Read widely. Pursue a variety of interests. Talk to folks
who seem to have exciting ideas.

You were born with the natural ability to create. But you might not
give your ideas and experiences enough room to buzz around in. Little
Mind has lots of rules about how you can put ideas together. Get out of
Little Mind and give the problem to Big Mind, which knows no rules
and will try any combination, just to see what happens. Big Mind is more
vast than any meadow, with worlds of room for bees and flowers. Little
Mind is about the size of a mayonnaise jar. If you trap your ideas in Little

Mind, they will surely die. Tear down the walls and the rules and let ideas spill all over each other.

Spam sandwich on wry — The Chinese Menu School of Creativity

In the wonderful film *The Apartment*, when Jack Lemmon prepares spaghetti for Shirley MacLaine, he uses his tennis racket as a strainer. It's a pity we don't get to see him serve the meatballs.

What ideas could you spawn by looking at that tennis racket from new perspectives? Eli Whitney got the idea for the cotton gin from seeing a cat trying to catch a chicken through a fence and coming up with a paw full of feathers. Creative thinkers play the "how many ways" and "how many uses" games all the time, on questions both significant and trivial, both practical and fanciful.

Getting sick of the same old lunch? How many new sandwich combinations could you create? Somebody had to invent the BLT, you know. Make a list of all the basic sandwich fillings you can think of. Then list all the condiments that come to mind. In a third list, note different breads and buns. Combining an element or elements from Column A with an element or elements from Column B and a bread from Column C, create a new sandwich sensation. My current favorite is peanut butter, red onion, shaved carrot and tomato on seven-grain bread.

Would you like to try writing the menu copy for that?

Writer Fran Striker created his Lone Ranger plots using this sort of grid technique, combining cattle rustlers, corrupt sheriffs and clever disguises in an almost-endless number of story combinations.

Porky Pig *is* Hamlet — What if Mel Blanc met William Shakespeare in show-business heaven?

"What if?" This simple question helps to unlock a Big Mind full of possibilities for creative problem solving.

What if everybody looked exactly alike?
What if no one ever told the truth?
What if the idea in golf was to take as many strokes as possible?
What if Peter Pan grew up?

Hmmmm. Intriguing notion. Let's play with it. What if Peter Pan grew up and forgot all about Neverland and became a corporate lawyer? What if he got himself a wife, two kids, a fancy house and a portable phone?

Silly questions? Maybe, but also multimillion-dollar ones when Steven Spielberg asked them. Those questions form the premise for *Hook*, Spielberg's blockbuster Christmas movie of 1991.

Everything that human beings created began as a "what if?"

What if you sliced up a potato and fried the slices in oil? You'd get an oil-saturated but nevertheless crispy and quite tasty concoction called, not the "oily fried potato slice," but the much more marketable "potato chip." Nobody thought to do that until 1865, and nobody thought to mass market the things until the A.A. Walter Company opened the first plant designed solely to make potato chips, in Albany, New York, in 1925. Imagine the world before the potato chip. The mind boggles.

Build a better potato chip and the world will come crunching to your door

"If it ain't broke, don't fix it," folk wisdom advises, so that little potato chip stayed pretty much the same for a long time. But then folks started fixing what wasn't broken, trying to get a competitive edge in the potato chip market. Chips began coming in flavors, and Ruffles gave them ridges, the better to hold the dip.

But unless you handled them very carefully, the chips tended to break into bits, and they got stale in the bag before you got to them. So the folks at Pringles decided to improve not the chip, but the container the chip comes in. The challenge: Develop a container that keeps the chips fresh and prevents them from crumbling.

How would you come up with such a container? Play with the notion.

You *could* try to improve the existing bag (steel-reinforced? with a combination lock?). But who says it has to be a bag at all? First you need to define the problem correctly. Your task isn't to come up with a better potato chip bag. The problem, properly defined, is to develop a better *container*, one that will keep the chips fresh and whole.

Time to free the bees. Let the pollination begin. Throw the discussion open to any and all possibilities.

How about a potato chip suitcase?

Could the chip come with its own protective wrapper, like the apple core, the banana peel or the eggshell?

How about a coffee can, tin can, tennis ball can. . . .

Tennis ball can. Hmmmmmmm. About the right size. Firm enough to hold up under buffeting from baggers at the supermarket. Vacuum sealed to keep the chips fresh.

You've just reinvented the Pringles potato chip can, the first innovation in chip packaging in decades. Had you gotten the idea a few years sooner, you could have made a major fortune.

As strong as the Rabbit of Gibraltar

Let's do one more exercise in creative fusion. Let's suppose you want to open an overnight mail delivery service. (An ironic choice in a book about slowing down.) You'd better be heavily capitalized (lots of money), as the competition is pretty fierce in the fast mail business these days. But you feel you can make it, if you can just get your message across to the public.

You want to develop a logo or symbol to convey the two strengths of your service: speed and dependability. (We like that in an overnight mail service, yes?) Where do you begin? By creating fusions, of course. Let's make two lists of symbols, one to represent speed, the other to represent dependability.

Images to represent speed
Mercury, winged feet, wings, a lightning bolt, the name set in *italic type* (which seems to suggest movement), a sprinter, maybe a famous sprinter, maybe Superman ("faster than a speeding bullet") or the Flash, a jet airplane (it wasn't that long ago we would have had to settle for a train, and before that, a galloping horse), snapping fingers ("in a snap"), a rabbit ("quick as a bunny"), a gunslinger ("fast on the draw"), a microwave oven, Madonna (wrong kind of fast?).

Images that express dependability
The Rock of Gibraltar, a bank vault, a safety deposit box, Mom, a rocking chair, a business suit, the family dog, the family dog bringing pipe and slippers, an elephant (never forgets), Donna Reed (or Harriet Nelson or June Cleaver . . .), Jimmy Stewart (as George Bailey).

Now take one from Column A and combine with one from Column B, another exercise from the Chinese Restaurant Menu School of Creativity. We get Mercury in a business suit, wings on the Rock of Gibraltar, a flying dog, a rabbit carrying pipe and slippers, an elephant in a field of lightning bolts, the Rabbit of Gibraltar. . . .

Any good ideas among this silliness? Could be. You probably won't be able to judge until you let the results sit for a while and come back to them in a more critical frame of mind. But that's for later. For now, be assured that this kind of thinking works, if you give it a little time.

You can develop a symbol that embraces contradictions (like fast stability) if you play at it. What could be more contradictory than "homey motel"? Motels are, by definition, not home. They're anonymous and homogenized. So how would you sell folks on the notion that your motel is homey? You start making fusions, and you come up with Tom Bodett promising to "leave the light on for you."

Life is like a hamburger

You've been combining words and symbols to create new images. If you'd like more work on making creative combinations and playing with possibilities, take a look at my two previous books from Writer's Digest Books: *Freeing Your Creativity* and *How to Write With the Skill of a Master and the Genius of a Child.*

For our purposes in learning to slow down and get more done, let's use the fusion technique to help you understand and define your approach to life. The words you use to describe your life in part determine how fully and powerfully you live. If your controlling metaphor for life is negative, it may limit your ability to create new possibilities for work, recreation and relationships. If you replace a negative metaphor with a positive one, you can empower yourself to approach life more creatively, can free yourself to make more and better choices.

Let's spend a little time uncovering and examining some of your controlling metaphors, applying the creative techniques we've just explored to the way you live.

Complete the following statement as many times as you can in three minutes. Write quickly. As a response jumps into your mind, write it down, without judging or analyzing. You don't even have to agree with the statement. Ready? Here's your sentence:

"Life is . . ."

Complete it any way you want, as many times as you can. Go.
Here are a few of the statements on my "life is . . ." list.

"Life is a bowl of cherries."
"Life is a game."
"Life is a journey."
"Life is a movie."
"Life is a mystery to be lived."
"Life is a problem to be solved."
"Life is a crap shoot."
"Life is dog eat dog."
"Life is meaningless."
"Life is a precious gift from God."

Take a look at your statements. Circle any that you agree with. You may circle statements that contradict one another. (We all hold contradictory beliefs.) Don't circle a statement because you think you *should* agree with it. Circle only those statements you *really* agree with.

See if any of the statements you've circled need amplification. For example, if you circled "Life is a movie," finish the statement:

"and I am the star."
"and I am the director."
"and I am the best boy [errand runner]."
"and I am a stunt player."
"and my part got left on the cutting-room floor."

If you circled "Life is a game," you might want to fill out the statement with:

"to be played for fun."
"to be won at any cost."
"without rules."

If you wrote that "Life is a journey," can you say where the journey leads?

Put a star by the statement that best defines your view of life at this moment. Go with your gut reaction here. Nobody has to know what you've selected, and you can always change your mind later.

What does your selection reveal? Does your metaphor empower you to make decisions and live your life fully? Or does the way you talk to yourself about life keep you from living as freely and fully as you might?

This isn't a matter of right and wrong. Your metaphor is true. But its opposite is true, too. Suppose you selected "Life is a problem to be solved." What could you gain from embracing a contrary statement, such as "Life is a game to be played" or "Life is a mystery to be lived"? Could this metaphor open you to another dimension of your own potential?

Find out. Write down a statement contrary to yours on a card and carry it around with you for a week. Pull the card out several times a day and read the statement. You won't convince yourself of its truth. You're simply reintroducing it to Little Mind, and giving Big Mind lots of chance to explore its possibilities. The new metaphor may open you up to new choices in the way you live each day.

"I am what I am"—is that *all* that I am?

Let's try the same sort of exercise to discover your controlling metaphor about yourself. Complete the following statement as many ways as you can in three minutes. Don't worry about being "accurate." Don't even worry about being serious. Allow yourself to play.

"I am . . . "

Go.

Set your list aside, and I'll share a little of mine. My first statements are quite mundane:

"I am forty-seven years old."
"I am a Caucasian male."
"I am married and have a son."
"I am a resident of Madison, Wisconsin."

But that still leaves two and a half minutes of "I am's" to go. Onward.

"I am a writer."
"I am a righter."
"I am a lefty politically."
"I am ambidextrous."
"I am color blind."
"I am several bubbles off of plumb."
"I am a voracious reader."
"I am determined."
"I am disciplined."
"I am difficult to live with."
"I am all the am's I ever was."
"I am new this minute."

And on, some silly, some maybe profound, some silly *and* profound. The sales copy for *Freeing Your Creativity* called me a "visionary." I rather like that, so I write that down, too.

Look at your list. Circle the "I am" you most strongly agree with. Circle, too, the "I am" that gives you the most pain when you acknowledge its truth. Try to determine which statement or statements affect the way you act. Do they empower or imprison you?

Again, embrace your opposite. If you have circled "I am dull," write "I am charismatic" or "I am dynamic." If you believe yourself to be entrapped, write "I am free." Practice reciting your new "I am." Do you see its truth?

Write an "I am" that most closely represents the way you'd *like* to be. Take some time with this if you need to. Carry this statement around with you and reread it often. What's to prevent you from becoming what that statement says you are? You won't become the reality simply by chanting the statement several times a day, but you can mentally and emotionally prepare yourself for the necessary changes. You can begin calling forth from your Big Mind the wisdom and the will you need to become the person you want to be.

If you can envision the reality and write it down on a card, you can embrace it and become it.

You can use this technique in other areas of your life, both to discover your controlling metaphor and, if you want, to change it. If your metaphor for your spouse is "ball and chain" or "warden," might it make a positive difference in your relationship if you changed the metaphor to "lover" or "soul mate"? If you think of the kids as "rug rats" or "tax deductions," could you improve your parenting by seeing them as "gifts from God" or "calls to love"?

We keep coming back to this central point:

Slow down.
Take the cleansing breath.

Instead of being controlled by internal, unconscious and thus automatic responses, shape the response you want to have to life. When you shape the response, you will shape the reality.

Owning it

Making time for fusions

Can you schedule creative and liberating thinking? Yes. You must. And no, you won't always get ideas when you're ready for them. You'll often get them when you least expect them.

Allow time in your daily life for the kind of exploring we've done here. If you have a problem, take time to define it properly. If you want to create a better can opener, rather than starting with the existing apparatus, play with the concept of "opening." If you're having troubles with your significant other, play with concepts of "relationship."

Gather the information you need (bees and flowers for your mental meadow). Then make as many unions as you can.

Where does time for this kind of thinking fit into your daily life? Maybe that's the wrong question. What happens if you redefine the problem this way: How can I live so that I'm constantly creative, and my days are filled with mental fusions?

Get in the habit of questioning assumptions constantly. If you find yourself thinking, "Says who?" a lot, you're on the right track. "We've always done it that way" is not a valid reason for doing it that way, and "We've never done it" is not a valid reason for not doing it.

Keep open to the brainstorm, the ah-ha! and the Eureka!—the answer or revelation that appears as sudden gift. You've been preparing to receive the gift through thought and effort, but you must turn the project over to Big Mind to dare to make the connections you need.

Embrace all your breakthroughs, even though many will turn out to be silly and impractical. Praise yourself for the creative genius you are. The more you encourage your unions, the more unions you'll have. The more you have, the more wonderful solutions you'll develop, the more beautiful stories you'll tell, the more authentic and free your life will become.

CHAPTER SEVENTEEN

Stress, time and the meaning of life

"Our inventions are wont to be pretty toys, which distract our attention from serious things. They are but improved means to an unimproved end."
HENRY DAVID THOREAU, *WALDEN*

Finding the courage to overcome speed sickness

Last night, I watched Bill Clinton, governor of Arkansas and one of several Democrats seeking his party's nomination for president, answer the questions put to him by Steve Croft, a reporter for "60 Minutes." The questions all concerned Clinton's fidelity (or lack thereof) to his marriage vows. Clinton's wife, Hillary, sat next to him during the interview and offered occasional comments.

Croft asked Clinton, in essence, "Have you ever cheated on your wife?"

Clinton responded to Croft, in essence, "None of your business."

To which Hillary Clinton added, in essence, "If folks don't like that answer, they should vote for somebody else."

Croft spent the remainder of the interview asking, in essence, "You're not really denying cheating on your wife, are you?"

This bizarre encounter came about because a tabloid supermarket "newspaper" published a "report" alleging that Clinton had been carrying on for twelve years with one Gennifer Flowers — whom I suspect will soon star in ads for skin-tight blue jeans, if she doesn't host her own talk show.

Whether you think the alleged extramarital affairs of presidential candidates to be any of your business, we clearly have a case of rights in conflict here. Croft has the right—even the obligation, given his chosen line of work—to ask questions. Clinton has the right to evade those questions, especially if the answers might incriminate him. And we the people have the right to watch or not watch Croft square off against Clinton, to judge the style and substance of the questions as well as the responses, and to plan our future television-watching and presidential-voting accordingly.

Meanwhile, in my town, the Ku Klux Klan has gotten a lot of play in the local press recently because of an alleged recruitment drive in nearby Beloit, Wisconsin, followed by the shocking revelation that a KKK chapter exists in Madison. Local leaders have expressed alarm and indignation and vow to "do something about it."

The Klan "chapter" turns out to be one antisocial individual with a phone answering machine that plays a barbaric message if you're foolish enough to call it. But the principle of rights in conflict remains. We have the right to organize into groups and to espouse any philosophy we choose. We also have the right to live free of racist, sexist and ageist harassment. My right to organize and to spout off my philosophy ends when my doing so violates your right to live free of me if you want to.

We have the right to join the Klan, to be outraged by the Klan, to ignore the Klan, to change the station to "Wheel of Fortune" when news of the Klan comes on.

Beneath all these rights in conflict, under all the struggles to be free, I believe that one fundamental freedom must abide.

The fundamental right from which all other rights derive: your right to decide what to do next.

That's what this book is all about. If someone has taken this most fundamental right from you, or if you've given it away, you must take it back if you would live free. We've explored lots of ways to do that.

We've focused especially on the speed sickness that seems to grip many of us these days and renders us unable to make those little decisions that add up to a life lived freely, on purpose. We travel too quickly to think and choose; our momentum carries us right past the off ramp before we can even read the sign.

Speed sickness isn't just "out there" in our hurry-up society. We've all absorbed it. Call it time pressure or stress, co-dependency or low self-esteem, Type A or workaholism—whatever you label it, the sickness is inside you, subverting your freedom from within.

As Walt Kelly, through his marvelous Pogo Possum, once observed, "We have seen the enemy, and it is us." You may have given away your fundamental freedom without a shot being fired.

It's time to reclaim your right to choose. That takes will. It takes awareness. It takes creativity. And it takes a great deal of courage. But you have all of these things, in abundance.

Teaching Norton to climb the stairs—A lesson in looking at the slats, not the gaps

As you know by now, my wife and I recently adopted two Persian kittens. Ralph is long and lean, with a pushed-in face and Oriental eyes. Norton is stocky (breeders call this body type "cobbie," which is nicer than calling him "fat," yes?), with a wide face and eyes that perpetually ask "Huh?" and "Who, me?"

Ralph is bold. Norton, alas, is considerably less so. Norton is so unbold, in fact, that for weeks he refused to try to go down our basement steps. The problem wasn't physical; Norton handled the stairs from the first floor to the second with, well, catlike ease. But the basement stairs were another, scarier story. On the unfinished basement stairs, he could see the gaps between the slats. He didn't see the sturdy, reliable steps. He saw the spaces between and, through those spaces, the headlines in the cat-tabloids:

Persian cat falls to death
Owners implicated in tragic accident
Abused cats—and the owners who claim to love them—
on the next "Geraldo"

Whatever he was seeing, Norton just wouldn't try those stairs. Ellen and I gave him "lessons," perching him on a step two or three rungs from the top and sitting on the landing, urging him up. His cries were pathetic.

I can empathize with Norton's timidity. I'm in many ways a fearless fellow. I can stand in front of a group of strangers and share my stories. I propel an automobile at 55 m.p.h. (and sometimes even a tick faster) among other automobiles driven by people I don't even know—many of whom are undoubtedly overstressed, tanked up, absent-minded or otherwise impaired—with hardly a thought for my own safety. I even drink water straight from the tap and eat at diners named "Bev's," "Dotty's" and "Mickey's."

But I'm just like Norton sometimes. I've got my own basement steps, challenges I'm afraid to meet, experiences I'm afraid to try, instances where I see the gaps and not the slats. And that's where I'm most apt to give away my previous freedom to the first taker, to let somebody else decide for me instead of grasping my freedom to decide, and with it, the responsibility to live by my decision.

Some fears are justified. Many are even helpful. I know a woman who says she never got started smoking cigarettes because she was afraid she'd look stupid holding the darn things. Her self-consciousness saved her from an addiction that's mighty tough to kick.

Many of our fears come from a valid assessment of our experiences. "Once burned, twice shy," the saying goes, and again, "Fool me once, shame on you. Fool me twice, shame on me." We learn, sometimes the hard way, not to dart out into traffic, not to stick our fingers into light sockets, not to try to draw to an inside straight.

But you know what Mark Twain said about the cat who jumped up on the hot stove, don't you? That cat will never jump on a hot stove again, but he'll never jump up on a cold one, either. Many of our fears aren't justified. And justified or not, they can paralyze us, rendering us unable to move up or down the stairs. Unless we take the time to examine our fears, we may never know the difference and will certainly never take the risks that lead not to disaster, but to new experience, new achievement, new joy.

How about you? What are your basement steps?

My story of Norton and the basement steps has a happy ending. One afternoon, as I was working through a set of bench presses in my basement "gym," I heard the scrabbling and jingling that indicates the near presence of a cat. When I looked up, expecting to see Ralph, I met instead Norton's steady, thoughtful gaze. Without fanfare and without assistance, he had overcome his fear. Perhaps his need to explore the basement grew stronger than his fear. Now Norton is free to roam throughout the house.

Unmasking the fear

Since we don't like to think of ourselves as cowards, we often disguise our fears, even from ourselves. Uncloak "I don't like parties," for example, and you may find "I'm afraid of people in groups of more than two." "I don't like to travel by airplane" may really mean "I don't really believe that heavy metal tube can fly, and certainly not with me sitting in it."

If you want to discover whether you harbor unacknowledged fears, first develop a list of people and actions you tend to avoid or feel some aversion toward. Take one of the items on your list and examine it closely, seeing if "don't want to" might mask "afraid to."

If you find a submerged fear, explore ways the fear may be keeping you trapped. Evaluate the rational concerns behind the fear. Suppose, for example, you discover that your fear of flying has prevented you from competing for a better job or taking a trip that could enrich your life. Evaluate that fear realistically. Find out the odds that you'll be hurt on a commercial air flight. How do those odds compare with driving a car? With taking a bath?

Decide whether you want to confront your fear and try to overcome it. You may decide to continue to shun travel by airplane, even though your research has led you to understand that, statistically, you're safer in an airplane than in your own bathtub. That's fine. Don't berate yourself for being "irrational." Of course you're irrational. That's part of being alive. But you'll have decided, and you'll know the reason why.

You may decide to try to overcome your fear and broaden your horizons. If so, figure out your next step and what you need to do to take it. Can you simply pick up the phone, call the travel agent, and set the process in motion? Or will you need help (more research, time to get used to the idea, a support group, therapy, hypnosis)?

You decide if you want and need to take the next step. You decide how to accomplish your goal. You take the responsibility for a misstep, and you enjoy the reward for the success.

What's it all for? Living a values-centered life

So far, our discussion has been value-neutral. We've talked about freeing up time, making decisions, taking risks, so you can do what you truly need and want to do. But these decisions aren't disconnected from their consequences, and you of course must judge those consequences and your intentions as you make your decisions.

One person wants to overcome a fear of flying to visit his Sainted Mother in the Old Country. Another wants to use airplane travel to increase her effectiveness as a sales representative. For a third, flying is an integral part of his plan to sell military secrets to Iraq. The courage required to overcome the fear of flying and the physical act of getting on the plane and buckling yourself in are the same in each case. But surely the purpose for and consequences of the action make a difference in how we evaluate the worth of that action.

Establishing your organizing principle

Recently Senator Al Gore wrote a book in which he says the United States needs to recognize the protection of our environment as the "organizing principle" for our society. We've had organizing principles in the past, he says. For example, in the 1950s, our organizing principle was defending against communism. We did a lot of things, from building a national highway system to bolstering the teaching of math and science in our schools, because of this organizing principle. Now, Gore says, we need to embrace the protection of the environment as our organizing principle.

How would your life change if we adopted Gore's principle?

I've encountered lots of other organizing principles in my life. When I was a Boy Scout, for example, I learned the organizing principle of service to God and country. I pledged to be trustworthy, loyal, helpful, friendly, courteous, kind, obedient, cheerful, thrifty, brave, clean and reverent, all in support of that principle of service.

Our country's organizing principle derives from its peoples' claim to the rights to "life, liberty, and the pursuit of happiness." Our government gets its power from the people, and any power the people don't expressly give to their government stays with them.

But as we've seen so often in our history, this basic principle gets defined and applied different ways in different times by different people. In the beginning, "people" meant white men who owned property. Decades passed before we recognized a black man as one of those "people," and still more decades before we allowed women to join the human race.

When the disciples asked Christ to get at the essence of the hundreds of Judaic laws governing behavior and the basic Ten Commandments Moses had given to the people, His reply was succinct: Love God with all your heart, mind and soul, and love your neighbor as yourself. But again, definition and application have varied throughout the ages, and the same Christian tenets have been used to justify both war and pacifism.

The fallacy of developing an organizing principle by consensus

Surely almost everyone would say that visiting your Sainted Mother in the Old Country is good, that selling military secrets to the enemy is bad, and that doing a better job of selling your product could be good or bad, depending on what you're selling, to whom, and for how much. If you decide with the majority, embracing the view held by "almost everyone," it doesn't necessarily make you right, but it probably makes you more comfortable.

But what "almost everybody" knows can change from day to day and depends on which "almost everybody" you're talking about. You must decide for you. If you find that your decision puts you in disagreement with 99 percent of those surveyed, that may make you lonely, but it doesn't make you wrong.

We all let ourselves be governed by what "everybody" knows sometimes. But when we do, we've given away the freedom to decide, which is the essence of a full, free and responsible life.

Is it important to know whether Bill Clinton fools around on his wife? Is it okay for you to run around on your spouse? Should you encourage other people to cheat on their mates? That's for you to decide. But it's important that you do decide, based on *your* organizing principle, on *your* underlying values.

Those underlying values and organizing principle give your life purpose and direction. They give you criteria for making decisions. When you establish your underlying values, making decisions becomes if not easy at least grounded. You can make a decision and keep to it.

When you express your fundamental values, you allow yourself to bring your actions into harmony with those values, eliminating the stress and uncertainty that develop when you act contrary to your basic beliefs.

I'm getting pretty lofty here, so I'll say it simply: You must know what you believe, and you must act on your beliefs.

Owning it

Developing your organizing principle

Almost every good business has a mission statement, usually as a part of its business plan. The mission statement guides the business through formation and growth. Unlike the procedures that govern day-to-day operations, the mission statement is a general statement of the reason for the business' existence.

Few individuals make a mission statement. Life is given to us. We don't have to develop a business plan, raise capital and file for incorporation. But a mission statement might help you develop your underlying principles, which in turn will help you make good decisions and understand the decisions you make. Creating your mission statement can help you to unplug from the automatic, unthinking response that comes with speed sickness.

If you think the project is worth exploring, take the time to develop your mission statement. It might begin this way:

"The fundamental purpose of my life is. . . ."

or

"I was placed on this earth to. . . ."

or

"The greatest good in my life is. . . ."

Allow yourself to roam freely through words, ideas, images. Try a lot of language. This is discovery, not an essay exam.

Your mission statement can take any form: a prose paragraph, a list, a rhyming couplet, a cartoon. Let the form serve what you want and need to express.

When you have your mission statement, set it aside. Let Little Mind sleep on it and Big Mind play with it. Come back to it another day and make any changes you might want.

Your organizing principle or principles flow from your mission statement and define who you are and how you choose to act. My organizing principles came out in the form of a list of ten "I will" statements. It isn't a wish list or New Year's resolutions. ("I will stop eating so many peanut butter chocolate chip cookies.") They are statements of what I *will* do, not what I intend or hope or wish to do.

My statements guide my decisions, serving as a template I can put over each day and each day's decisions.

My first three statements reflect my belief in and concept of God.

My fourth statement is, "I will seek to learn." That doesn't mean I will within the next year take a specific number of credit courses or noncredit workshops, read a certain number of books, attend lectures, or watch "Nova" and "Nature" on PBS (although I may very well do most of those things). It means I will read and listen, ask and question; that I will be open in my ignorance, that I'll recognize other people's ability to teach me their unique truths, based on their experiences.

My seventh statement sounds pretty combative but shouldn't surprise you by now: "I will question everything and decide for myself."

The next statement has a more reconciliatory tone: "I will seek always to understand the other person's perspective." The tenth is a declaration of peace upon the world, ending with, "I will unplug my temper response."

I'm not sure I could explain or justify my statements to you. I don't have to. They're for me. But I'm accountable to you for any action I take that affects you.

I know I won't always live up to my organizing principles. They're a guide designed to help me, not yet another occasion for judging myself unworthy. I can change them any time they no longer serve me.

If you think it would be helpful, take time now to create your own underlying principle or principles, as a guide to future decision making.

One more look at the basic principles of the slow-down life

We began this book with a mission statement and established organizing principles throughout. The mission statement is the title of the book: *Slow Down . . . and Get More Done*. Put another way, I'm urging you to reclaim your life.

These statements contain several assumptions:

- You may be somewhat out of control of your life because you move too quickly and make decisions reflexively.
- Your life is worth reclaiming.
- You can reclaim your life by slowing down.
- You possess the power to do so.

Out of that mission statement and its assumptions flowed a couple of basic organizing principles and several smaller principles of behavior. Here are the two most important principles, rephrased in "I will" statements:

I will decide how to spend my time. I will have the courage to be nobody but myself.

Principles of behavior

1. I will accept the consequences and pay the price promptly for my decisions.
2. I will stay open to the possibilities in each moment.
3. I will listen to my intuitions.
4. I will treat myself at least as well as I'd treat the family dog.
5. I will act instead of worrying about acting.
6. I will banish the distracters from my life.
7. I will accept waiting as an opportunity for rest and reflection.
8. I will seek right work and make work right.
9. I will seek the rest and respite I need.
10. I will exercise and eat to enhance my health and well-being.
11. I will nurture and rejoice in my creative power.

How many of those principles are you ready to adopt as your own? How would you change them? Which principles will you add?

Only you can create your answers. Only you can live by them. Let them guide your life. If you do, you will never violate your truth.

When in doubt, stop, take the cleansing breath, and remind yourself of why you're living and what you hope to accomplish with your life. Then you'll be ready to decide and act.

BIBLIOGRAPHY

Books that fed this book

In chapter fourteen I shared with you a few of the books that have shaped my perceptions. Now I give you a more specific and focused list of books, some of the ones that contributed directly to the book you've just read. I'll list them by subject and give a brief summary, a map for your further exploration on these subjects.

Time-management
How to Get Control of Your Time and Your Life
Alan Lakein; Peter H. Wyden, publisher, 1973.

Still probably the best and one of the most humane books on the subject.

How to Live on 24 Hours a Day
Arnold Bennett; Doubleday, 1910.

To Bennett, the supply of time is a daily miracle. You have always had all the time there is, he reminds us, and suggests you put it to good use by reading, reflecting and learning.

Get It All Done and Still Be Human: A Personal Time-Management Workshop
Tony and Robbie Fanning; Chilton Book Company, 1979.

The Fannings remind you that life isn't just little boxes to check. You should aim to feel good and not just to do more. They remind you that "I don't have time" really means "I choose to do other things" or "I don't want to."

Manage Your Time, Manage Your Work, Manage Yourself
Merrill E. and Donna M. Douglass; AMACOM, 1980.

What a shame they felt the need to tell us to "declare war on ourselves."

The Time Trap
Alec Mackenzie; AMACOM, 1990 (first published 1972).

Good on helping you to say "no."

How to Cure Yourself of Positive Thinking
Donald G. Smith; Seemann Publishing, 1976.

A savage attack on all the false claims on your time. You don't have to do anything that is unpleasant or unnecessary, Smith asserts. Eliminate these wasters, and the sheer joy of being alive will emerge.

The Ninety-Minute Hour
Jay Conrad Levinson; E.P. Dutton, 1990.

I was pretty horrified by the image of life I encountered here. To me this is time-management gone amuck.

Timesource
Paul Rice; Ten Speed Press, 1989.

Time-management goes "new age." Rice brings biorhythms and Seasonal Affective Disorder into the mix and breaks time into a number of subcategories, such as listening time, decision time and communication time.

Timelock: How Life Got So Hectic and What You Can Do About It
Ralph Keyes; HarperCollins, 1991.

Another "new age" book and an excellent approach. The harder you try to control time, Keyes says, the more it controls you. Reduce the amount of stuff you try to cram into the available time, he advises. Become less concerned about time; focus instead on living.

The Harried Leisure Class
Staffan Burenstam Linder; Columbia University Press, 1970.

Affluence has not freed us, Linder says. Instead, more money has resulted in our working harder for still more money.

For grounding on how we brought the age of impatience on ourselves, you might also read any of the time studies written by John Robinson. For an economic foundation for your new simplified life, read E.F. Schumacher's 1973 classic *Small Is Beautiful*, subtitled "economics as if people mattered" (Harper & Row).

Stress and health
Mind as Healer, Mind as Slayer: A Holistic Approach to Preventing Stress Disorders
Kenneth R. Pelletier; Delacorte Press, 1977.

Dr. Pelletier explains stress as an internal response of the body, a natural coping mechanism that has become excessive and thus harmful. Pelletier also shows the link between emotion and a whole host of plagues, including cancer, rheumatoid arthritis and migraine headache. This fine book will help you understand and deal effectively with your own stress reactions.

The Healing Heart: Antidotes to Panic and Helplessness
Norman Cousins; Norton, 1983.

Cousins documents with his own experience the healing value of laughter, hope, faith and love, along with confidence and great expectations. Read also his *Anatomy of an Illness*.

If you want to go directly to the primary source on stress, read Hans Selye, *Stress Without Distress* (Lippincott, 1974) and *The Stress of Life* (McGraw-Hill, 1978).

Stress and the work place
Healthy People in Unhealthy Places: Stress and Fitness at Work
Kenneth R. Pelletier; Delacorte Press, 1984.

Here's verification, from a compassionate doctor, of something you may have already known by instinct: Your work, and the stress it produces in you, can make you sick. Good, clear definitions and explorations of workaholism and Type-A behavior. Pelletier will help you understand the sickness and begin to get well.

The Three Boxes of Life—And How to Get Out of Them: An Introduction to Life/Work Planning
Richard Nelson Bolles; Ten Speed Press, 1981.

We've segmented life into three discrete chunks, Bolles says: learning, working, and retiring/playing. He shows why that's a crazy way to live and offers help in breaking down those barriers, so we can learn, work and play throughout life.

Adaptation to Life
George E. Vaillant; Little, Brown, 1977.

If you want to understand health, study healthy people, Vaillant says. You can master conflict creatively, and this book can help.

Sleep
No More Sleepless Nights
Peter Hauri and Shirley Linde; John Wiley & Sons, 1990.

The classic in the field. Hauri directs the insomnia program at the Mayo Clinic. In this book, he and Linde help you to "be your own sleep therapist."

For more information on sleep, call The American Sleep Disorders Association in Rochester, Minnesota: (507) 287-6006.

Talk-back therapy
Feeling Good: The New Mood Therapy
David D. Burns; Morrow, 1980.

A step-by-step process for uncovering the covert, negative recordings we play to ourselves and learning to talk back to them. If you go with the process and really "do" this book, it can be a revelation.

A New Guide to Rational Living
Albert Ellis and Robert A. Harper; Prentice-Hall, 1975.

Another good book on "deprogramming" or "depropagandizing" your-self from self-defeating beliefs. You don't need to judge or rate yourself, the authors advise.

How I Found Freedom in an Unfree World
Harry Browne; Macmillan, 1973.

You can choose to live your life as you want, without having to change the world or other people. Simplify. Start from zero. Set your own stan-dards. Nobody can grant you freedom. It isn't anybody else's to give.

The Seven Habits of Highly Effective People: Restoring the Character Ethic
Stephen R. Covey; Fireside, Simon & Schuster, 1989.

Covey offers no quick fix, no cosmetic surgery, but instead a way of examining and shaping the basic principles you live by. "Are you living or being lived?" he asks. "You can choose your response."

Being yourself
Passages: Predictable Crises of Adult Life
Gail Sheehy; Dutton, 1976.

A classic. The narrow, dissembling self must die, Sheehy insists. Often we require a crisis to learn this. We are happiest when we use all of our capacities, fully integrated. You can't hurry up and find yourself. It's a gradual unfolding, and it's never finished.

Notes on How to Live in the World . . . and Still Be Happy
Hugh Prather; Doubleday, 1986.

Ego is a shabby self-image we create out of fear, Prather says. Don't respond out of ego; act out of kindness and love. Ego assumes anything in the future is more important than what you're doing now, and any-thing in the past is more real than what you're doing now. Heart lives in the present; follow your heart. Ego bids you to hurry. Go slowly. A wise and gentle book.

The Wisdom of Insecurity
Alan Watts; Pantheon, 1951.

We fail to live, Watts tells us, because we're always preparing to live. We seek security and painlessness, which denies our life. "Life, change, movement and insecurity are so many names for the same thing," Watts says. You can only live in the present, guided by the real wisdom of the body. Another beautiful guide.

Healing Journey: The Odyssey of an Uncommon Athlete
David Smith, with Franklin Russell; Sierra Club Books, 1983.

"Failure is always orchestrated from within," Smith tells us. "We sit within the powerhouse of self . . . frightened to let out our creativity, lest we discover ourselves." Smith will help you set yourself free.

On the same path, read also *Zen in the Art of Archery*, by Eugene Herrigel (Pantheon, 1953).

All God's Children Are Lost, But Only a Few Can Play the Piano: Finding a Life That is Truly Your Own
Sheldon Kopp; Prentice-Hall, 1991.

Honor your peculiarities to find the higher power within you, Kopp says. Choose to live by your own values and desires. Let go of the old to discover what comes next. Everybody wants to go to heaven, he reminds us, but nobody wants to die.

The Body Is the Hero
Ronald J. Glasser; Random House, 1976.

Explore your opposites. Embrace playfulness.

A Gift from the Sea
Anne Morrow Lindbergh; Vintage, 1991 (1955).

When Morrow added a chapter for the 1983 revision, she seemed amazed that people were still reading her quiet classic. If you read it, you'll know why. Particularly good in discussing the unique pressures women face, but Lindbergh can help anyone find peace and serenity in solitude.

Chronicles of a Rural Journalist in America
Norbert Blei; Samizdat Press, 1990.

If you want more on the life and times of "the most dangerous journalist in America," you can go straight to the coyote's mouth.

Worry
Not to Worry
Mary McClure Goulding and Robert L. Goulding; Silver Arrow/William Morrow, 1989.

Worry is a learned response, and the worry addiction is curable. The authors detail causes of worry—including worrying because everything is going just fine—and suggest a means of escape.

Finding right work
Do What You Love, the Money Will Follow: Developing Your Right Livelihood
Marsha Sinetar; Paulist Press, 1987.

You must first like yourself, Sinetar advises, to choose what is right and true for you. Then you must follow your heart to find your right livelihood. The right way is not necessarily the easy way, she warns. But if you find work to match your disposition and aptitude, the work will be its own reward, it will nourish you, and you will succeed at it. A liberating book.

Good Work
E.F. Schumacher; Harper & Row, 1979.

It isn't work that stresses, Schumacher says. It's wrong work for wrong reasons. There can be no joy of life, he says, without joy of work. And yet we have educated ourselves for leisure, not for work, and industrialization has led to dull, meaningless work.

Follow Your Bliss
Hal Zina Bennett and Susan Sparrow; Avon, 1990.

You must listen to your true voice, guiding you to what you love. Your true voice is calm, peaceful, centered; it produces "a quiet excitement." It's a trustworthy guide. False voices are anxious and strident.

Work and Human Behavior
Walter S. Neff; Aldine, 1985.

This is a good source of material—both historical and in the present—on our attitudes toward work. Based on all his factual grounding, Neff contends that mental and physical health are a function of the "goodness of fit" between you and your work.

Confessions of a Workaholic: The Facts About Work Addiction
Wayne Oates; World Publishing/Times Mirror, 1971

Oates clearly defines workaholism, explains why we suffer from it and how we can recover. Rest is a natural part of creation, he tells us, and work without satisfaction is like salt water, never quenching thirst.

The Overworked American: The Unexpected Decline of Leisure
Juliet B. Schor; Basic Books, 1991.

Schor explains how we traded time for money and got trapped in the earn-spend cycle.

Creativity
The Act of Creation
Arthur Koestler; Macmillan, 1964.

A rich, complex book of life, describing creativity as a fusion of disparate elements.

Writing Down the Bones: Freeing the Writer Within
Natalie Goldberg; Shambhala, 1986.

I'd read dozens of books about writing, and I didn't think another one could get me excited all over again the way this one did. Goldberg showed me that I'd been writing with the brakes on.

The Three-Pound Universe
Judith Hooper and Dick Teresi; Macmillan, 1986.

A readable and fascinating journey through the maze of theories on how the brain works. You'll learn all about the brain, but the mind will remain a mystery, as the authors freely admit.

A Whack on the Side of the Head
Roger von Oech, Warner Books, 1990 (1983).

The subtitle is audacious: *How You Can Be More Creative*. Oech will help jump-start you by getting you to look at things from different angles. See also von Oech's *A Kick in the Seat of the Pants* (Perennial Library, 1986) and a little deck of creativity cards he calls his "Creative whack pack."

Chuck Amuck: The Life and Times of an Animated Cartoonist
Chuck Jones; Farrar, Straus & Giroux, 1989.

Father of Bugs Bunny and the Roadrunner. Creativity requires freedom and a lack of critical judgment, positive or negative. You'll catch the spirit from Jones.

The Zen of Seeing: Seeing/Drawing as Meditation
Frederick Franck; Vintage, 1973.

Before Betty Edwards taught us how to draw with the right side of our brains, Franck taught the quiet wisdom of getting out of the way. Really see the object, and then lose yourself in it. This book is for all of us, not just for artists.

INDEX